Imbert de Saint-Amand

Marie Antoinette and the end of the old regime

Imbert de Saint-Amand

Marie Antoinette and the end of the old regime

ISBN/EAN: 9783742842640

Manufactured in Europe, USA, Canada, Australia, Japa

Cover: Foto ©Andreas Hilbeck / pixelio.de

Manufactured and distributed by brebook publishing software (www.brebook.com)

Imbert de Saint-Amand

Marie Antoinette and the end of the old regime

MARIE ANTOINETTE

AND

THE END OF THE OLD RÉGIME

BY

IMBERT DE SAINT-AMAND

TRANSLATED BY

THOMAS SERGEANT PERRY

WITH PORTRAIT

SECOND EDITION

LONDON
HUTCHINSON & CO.
25, Paternoster Square
1892

CONTENTS.

	PAGE
INTRODUCTION	1

CHAPTER		
I.	THE BIRTH OF THE DAUPHIN	13
II.	THE GRAND DUKE PAUL AT VERSAILLES	21
III.	"THE MARRIAGE OF FIGARO"	31
IV.	GUSTAVUS III. AT VERSAILLES	43
V.	"THE BARBER OF SEVILLE" AT THE TRIANON	51
VI.	THE CARDINAL DE ROHAN	60
VII.	CAGLIOSTRO	68
VIII.	THE COUNTESS DE LA MOTTE	76
IX.	THE NECKLACE	86
X.	THE ARREST	95
XI.	THE TRIAL	104
XII.	THE VERDICT	115
XIII.	A PICTURE OF MADAME LEBRUN'S	128
XIV.	MADAME ELISABETH AT MONTREUIL	135
XV.	CAZOTTE'S PROPHECY	150
XVI.	THE BEGINNING OF THE REVOLUTION	160
XVII.	THE ASSEMBLY OF NOTABLES	168
XVIII.	THE PROCESSION OF MAY 4, 1789	181

CHAPTER		PAGE
XIX.	THE OPENING SESSION OF THE STATES-GENERAL	188
XX.	THE DEATH OF THE DAUPHIN	196
XXI.	THE ADVANCE OF THE REVOLUTION	201
XXII.	THE DEPARTURE OF THE DUCHESS OF POLIGNAC	213
XXIII.	THE QUEEN AND THE MARQUIS OF LA FAYETTE	222
XXIV.	MARIE ANTOINETTE AND THE DUKE OF ORLEANS	230
XXV.	THE BANQUET OF OCTOBER 1	241
XXVI.	THE FIFTH OF OCTOBER	246
XXVII.	THE SIXTH OF OCTOBER	257
	EPILOGUE	270

MARIE ANTOINETTE

AND

THE END OF THE OLD RÉGIME

MARIE ANTOINETTE

AND

THE END OF THE OLD RÉGIME,

1781–1789.

INTRODUCTION.

THE old régime is drawing to its close; the hour of the great catastrophes is nigh; soon the deep roar of thunder is to be heard; yet, so far as appears, nothing is changed: the splendor of Versailles still dazzles every eye by its magnificence; everywhere one sees the same life, the same animation, the same brilliancy. There are nearly four thousand persons in the King's civil household, nine or ten thousand in his military household, and at least two thousand more in those of his relatives. There is a vast accumulation of rich costumes, of uniforms, liveries, coaches. How beautiful is the park of Versailles on a spring morning, when the chestnuts are in blossom, and the sun lights up the spray of the great fountains! The terrace is crowded with women richly dressed, and with men quite as gorgeously arrayed, in their knots of ribbons, their lace ruffles, and their yellow, or pink, or sky-blue silk coats. The military bands are playing beneath the trees. One may see the Swiss Guards in their sixteenth century uniforms, with their halberds, ruffs, plumed hats, and full jerkins of various colors; the body-guards with their red breeches, huge boots, and blue coats adorned with white embroidery. One beholds, too, the crowd of courtiers with their attentive, discreet air, with the distinction of their gait, speech, and smile, with their reverence for etiquette, and their boundless courtesy.

Let us imagine ourselves at the last court balls of 1786 and 1787. The place is the small theatre between the Court of the Princes and the park where the southern part of the palace begins. The building, which was constructed under Louis XIV., but is now destroyed, is thus described by the Count d' Hézecques in his *Memories of a Page*. It was fitted out with wooden pavilions, which were kept in the house of the Menus Plaisirs, and can be set up in a few hours. The entrance was in a green grove, adorned with statues, and at the end was a billiard room, which was a little sombre in color, so that the illumination shone out with greater brilliancy. To the right, small paths lead into the dancing and gaming room. One of the doors consists of a great piece of plate glass so clear that a Swiss sentinel is posted there to warn people from trying to walk through it. Marble basins, surrounded with moss and flowers, contain water-jets which splash all night, in the brilliant blaze of lamps and candles, giving forth an agreeable coolness. The guests at these delightful balls are the most distinguished, the most attractive people of the fascinating society that sets the fashion for all Europe. M. Taine thus describes their charms, with real enthusiasm, in his noble book, *The Origins of Contemporary France*: "There is not a toilette here, not a pose of the head, not a tone of the voice, which is not the fine flower of worldly culture, the distilled essence of the most exquisite products of social art. It takes, we are told, a hundred thousand roses to produce an ounce of that unique ottar which the kings of Persia use. This drawing-room is like that, a minute flash of gold and crystal. It contains the substance of a human vegetation. To fill it, there was required a great aristocracy transplanted into a hothouse and so rendered sterile of fruits, though rich in flowers, in order that in the royal alembic all its purified juices should be concentrated into a few drops of perfume. Its cost is most extravagant, but only in that way are delicate perfumes made."

Up to its last moment, the monarchy was imposing. The royal star, before it disappeared beneath the horizon, continued to shine in great splendor. Chateaubriand was presented at court May 19, 1787, and he thus describes the occasion: "No one has seen anything who has not seen the pomp of Versailles, even after the disbanding of the King's former household. It is because Louis XIV. is always here. Hence a presentation is not a thing of trifling importance. A mysterious destiny hangs over the new arrival. He is spared that air of scornful protection, which with extreme politeness forms the inimitable manners of the great nobleman. Who knows whether this newcomer may not become the master's favorite?" The doors of the King's bedchamber are opened, and the King, who has just finished dressing, takes his hat from the hand of the first gentleman in waiting, and comes forth to go to mass. The future author of *The Martyrs* bows. The Marshal de Duras pronounces his name, "Sire, the Chevalier de Chateaubriand"; and the famous author, recalling this memory of his youth, says: "Vanity of human destiny! This sovereign whom I saw for the first time, this mighty monarch, was Louis XVI., then within six years of the scaffold; and this new courtier, at whom he scarcely glanced, commissioned to separate bones from bones, after having been presented to the grandeur of the descendant of Saint Louis, on proving his titles to nobility, was to be again presented to his ashes, on proving his fidelity — a twofold tribute of respect to the twofold royalty of the sceptre and of the martyr's palm."

After his presentation to Louis XVI., Chateaubriand passed through the gallery to meet the Queen returning from chapel. "She soon came in sight," he says, "surrounded by a large and brilliant suite; she made a dignified courtesy, appearing enchanted with life. And those fair hands, which then held so gracefully the sceptre of so many kings, were, before they were tied by the executioner, to patch the rags of the widow, the prisoner of the Conciergerie."

Unhappy Queen! The moment was drawing nigh when she was to be abandoned even by her courtiers. At the last court ball in 1788, no one wanted to dance with her. Madame Vigée-Lebrun, who was present, speaks of the festivity most sadly: "The box in which I happened to be was so near the Queen's that I could overhear what she said. I saw her in some agitation inviting the young men of the court to dance, among them, M. de Lameth, who belonged to a family which she had overwhelmed with deeds of kindness, and others, who refused her; so that it was impossible to make up the sets for the square dances. The indecorous conduct of these gentlemen struck me; their refusal seemed to me to be a sort of revolt. The Revolution was approaching; it broke out the next year."

In 1787 Marie Antoinette had already noticed threatening symptoms. In the *Secret Correspondence*, published by M. de Lescure, there may be read, under date of February 19: "Last week the Queen was much applauded when she reached the Opera; and, as usual, she made courtesies to the public. At that moment a hiss was heard from the crowd. Although this piece of insolence must have come from a madman or a wretch, it much distressed the Queen." Certainly he was right, for that hiss at the Opera was the first sound of the most horrible tempest.

In the same *Correspondence*, under the date of August 1, 1787, we find: "The name of Madame Deficit is given to a great lady who has made certain sacrifices to the nation which was in no way authorized to demand them." And, September 25, "'Athalie' was recently played in Paris. The public applauded with as much warmth as indecorum these four lines: —

> "'Confound in her designs this cruel queen!
> Deign, deign, my God, on Mathan and on her
> To let fall that spirit of imprudence and error,
> The fatal foreteller of the ruin of kings.'"

The moment chosen for this ill-will towards Marie Antoinette was the very one when she had abandoned these faults and had become serious and exemplary. We find, again, in the *Secret Correspondence*, December 5, 1786, this sign of growing gravity: "The Revolution, which has been so long prophesied at our court, is beginning to show itself. The Queen turns a cold shoulder to all the young men who had assumed an air of familiarity which seemed justified by the destruction of all etiquette. She admits to her society only reasonable and decent men, if such there be. All the high officers and servants of the King and the Princes are to be obliged to live at Versailles. In this way, Œil-de-Bœuf and this gallery, which were deserted, will be crowded again. It is supposed that the Queen is becoming devout. She would thus follow her mother's example at an early age."

So long as Marie Antoinette was frivolous and was

guilty, not of real faults, but of imprudent actions, she was the recipient of general flattery and admiration. But so soon as she became absolutely irreproachable, she was overwhelmed with harsh judgments and ill-will. Such is the world's justice!

The same thing may be said about the nobility. As M. Taine has justly remarked, never was the aristocracy so worthy of power as at the moment when it was about to lose it. The possessors of privileges had become excellent citizens, worthy, enlightened, charitable managers. They defended the tax-payers from the treasury, suppressed the duty service, multiplied good works, taught the poor, protected agriculture, directed every reform.

Turn to the memorials of the nobility prepared in the bailiwicks on the eve of the States-General, and you will see that they demanded for the French people all the civil and political rights which the Revolutionists pretend to have wrung from them. These great lords, who fought in the war like heroes, and at Versailles so well represented the splendors of the past, were, in their own homes, the most amiable of hosts, the most delicate patrons of letters and the arts, the sturdiest supporters of the new ideas. They were rich, but they were generous; they were envied by the ungrateful, but noble hearts blessed them.

The Viscountess of Noailles said with much truth: " The horror of abuses, the contempt of hereditary distinctions, all those feelings with which a sense of their own interest inspired the lower classes, acquired their first charm from the enthusiasm of the great. Those of lively imaginations hoped soon to see their wildest dreams come true, or gladly deprived themselves of everything of the nature of an abuse, in the simple thought that they should thus attain a moral height which the masses would be generous enough to understand and to respect."[1] Going back to the Golden Age of the Revolution, she exclaims: "Heaven knows how unjust we are to that time! What generosity, loftiness, delicacy, belonged to that distinguished society! How solid was every tie! What respect for sworn fidelity, even in the unworthiest circumstances! Never has romance so manifested itself in life as then. I know it is precisely the reproach, and a well-founded reproach, that can be made against this society, that it lacked moral poise to an extent that left a vagueness perilous to virtue. But is not that the general spirit of the century?"

The whirl of new ideas, the general animation and fervor, made conversation varied, witty, and eloquent. The differences of opinion struck out sparks of brilliant wit. The French nobility, though old in certain ways, had remained young in others. Yes, even when the old régime was in its agony, it was still young in ardor, courage, and hope. It was young because it believed in love, and because it did

---

[1] *Life of the Princess of Poix née Beauveau*, by the Viscountess of Noailles (born in 1791; died in 1851).

not know the general disenchantment, the despairing scepticism, the disgust with life which are the shame and the punishment of decadent society. It was to fall, but gracefully, easily, like an ancient gladiator, delighted to unite in its last years all its qualities, all its charms, as if to make itself missed and to permit Prince Talleyrand to be able to say, " No one who did not live before 1789 has any idea of the charm of life."

"Gaiety," wrote an English tourist in 1785, "is a peculiar quality of the French." This good humor, this singular combination of irony and excitement, of indifference and enthusiasm, the French nobility preserved up to the time of their severest trials. It seemed as if, knowing their days were numbered, they were anxious to pass them joyfully, to multiply their pleasures, their adventures, their emotions, as much as possible. To those who prophesied the approaching calamities, they answered with an incredulous smile. As Madame de Genlis said, their feeling of security amounted to extravagance.

June 29, 1789, at a meeting of the King's Council at Marly, Necker said very innocently (for this society was perhaps even more innocent than refined): "What could be idler than fears about the organization of the States-General? They can do nothing without the King's assent." Was not the Revolution, in their eyes, like a vast lottery in which every one imagines that he has a winning ticket? What could happen, thought the nobles, even if the worst should arrive? A little war, gentle and charming, like that of the Fronde. No long campaigns or tedious manœuvres. A few sharp thrusts, and fiddles, balls, comedies, love affairs, and songs, and, afterwards, wise reconciliation, useful reforms, progress, philanthropy, the triumph of tender souls, the progress of humanity! We shall speak, shouted the lawyers, who are always ready to speak; we shall ascend the tribune, we shall become famous and be appointed ministers. We shall make money, said the financiers. And financiers favor revolutions; for, as a clever woman of the time said, discount forms more than a third part of a banker's opinions.

All forms of amusement followed one another with giddy rapidity. Fashionable men and women lived a double life, now in Paris, now at Versailles. A steady stream of carriages with swift horses was rolling incessantly from the city of the great King to the real capital, that of pleasure and public opinion. At Versailles etiquette still ruled; in Paris there was freedom. There were delightful suppers, such as Madame Oberkirch describes: "Without wit, without eloquence, without knowledge of the world, of good stories, of the thousand trifles which make up the news of the day, no one could dream of being admitted to these charming gatherings. Only there was there any conversation, and it was on the most trifling subjects; it was all a mere foam that was evaporating fast, leaving no trace behind, but its taste was most agreeable. After once tasting it, everything else seemed flat." There were the plays in which politics mingled with literature, and the audience was more interesting than the performance. There were private theatricals in which the most serious professions furnished excellent comedians; many judges took the parts of Crispin and Marcarille. Great ladies, actresses, demi-reps, made great show of luxury, and without associating together, had yet perfect knowledge of one another's deeds and actions. Among the fashionable promenades was the Boulevard du Temple, where, especially on Thursday, men used to ride; the large avenue of the Tuileries, and besides, to the left of the Palais Royal, another equally famous rideway, where good company was wont to assemble in gorgeous dress. In summer this was a favorite resort after the theatre; the women used to carry huge bouquets which, in combination with the perfumed powder they put on their hair, rendered the air most fragrant. There they used sometimes to sit till two in the morning, listening to harps and guitars. Saint Georges would take his violin there, and Garat and Alsévédo would sing, giving an improvised, open-air concert in the moonlight. The French nobility, which was as admirable at a ball as on the battle-field, generous with its heart's blood and its money, which greeted the first rays of rising freedom, was to maintain its dignity to the last. Even in prison, even before the court, even on the platform of the guillotine, it was to remain what it had been,—amiable, courteous, *comme il faut*. Of the

Conciergerie it was to make a drawing-room; at the end of a corridor in which four candles were burning, it was to compose madrigals and songs, and continue as gallant, as gay, as graceful as before. Is there any need of becoming cross and sullen because you are detained by accident in a wretched inn?

Yet, even behind bolts, the women will keep alive the holy fire of fashion, the charm of elegance, and the prison-court will resemble a flowery terrace set in a framework of iron. To quote from Count Beugnot, himself a prisoner in the Conciergerie: "There misfortune will be treated like a naughty child who has to be laughed at, and in fact the divinity of Marat, the priesthood of Robespierre, the magistracy of Fouquier-Tinville will be loudly laughed at, and all will seem to say to the bloody gang: 'You may kill us when you please, but you can't prevent our being amiable!'" French nobles, you will not only be gentle, you will be courteous with death! After knowing how to live, you will know how to die, and you will find a way to honor the scaffold by leaving upon it your coat-of-arms!

I.

THE BIRTH OF THE DAUPHIN.

THE most touching thing in the world is the suffering and then the joy of a woman who gives birth to a child. Those tortures endured with so much courage, the anguish so distressing to the husband or the mother, that waiting in which minutes seem like centuries, the solemn moment in which the woman seems to hang between hope and death; then the ineffable, ecstatic joy, the heavenly rest, that sweetest of sounds, the child's first cry, the first look the mother gives it; — what is sublimer than the mystery of birth, than the living poem of maternal love, than this outburst of the deepest and truest feelings of nature? The day for which Marie Antoinette had so longed was at last come, and Heaven granted her the immense happiness of giving a Dauphin to France and to the King. Poor Louis XVI., whose lot was soon to be so piteous, with what love one saw his happiness! with what sympathy were regarded the tears of joy that bedewed his honest and loyal face!

It was October 22, 1781; the whole palace of Versailles was agitated by the liveliest emotions. It was one in the afternoon when a Dauphin was born. On this occasion there had been abandoned the old barbaric custom of letting a crowd fill the Queen's room, and only a few persons had been admitted. At first they refrained from telling the Queen that it was a Dauphin, lest the excitement should be too great for her. She noticed their silence, and supposed it was a girl. "See how reasonable I am," she said; "I don't ask any questions." The King did not wish to prolong her uncertainty, and called out, "The Dauphin asks leave to enter." At these words the tender, — dare I say happy? yes, for at this moment she was, — happy Marie Antoinette lifted herself up, held out her arms to the King, and then the couple, closely embracing, mingled their tears, which were so delicious that the Dauphin lay for some moments by their side before they noticed him.

As a Swede, the Count of Stedingk, said, the Queen's ante-chamber was a charming sight. The joy was complete; every head was turned, and all were alternately weeping and laughing. Men and women who were scarcely acquainted found themselves hugging one another. But it was very different when, at two o'clock, the door of the Queen's room was thrown wide open and the Dauphin was announced! The governess of the royal children, the Princess of Guéménée, held the little child in her arms. The applause and the clapping of hands made their way to Marie Antoinette's chamber, and certainly to her heart. An archbishop wanted the

Dauphin to be at once invested with the order of the Holy Ghost. "No," said the King; "he must first be made a Christian." At three o'clock the child was baptized in the chapel of the palace by the Grand Almoner, the Cardinal de Rohan. He was held at the font by the Count of Provence and by Madame Elisabeth, who represented the godfathers and godmothers, the Emperor Joseph II. and the Princess of Piedmont (Madame Clotilde). In his joy, Louis XVI. gave his hand to every one, taking every opportunity to say, "My son" or "The Dauphin." In the streets all were talking and embracing one another. All classes of society, from the highest to the lowest, seemed to form one happy family.

Madame Elisabeth's friend, Madame de Bombelles, wrote to her husband on the day of the Dauphin's birth: "What touched me extremely was the King's delight during the baptism; he was continually looking at his son and smiling at him. The cries of the people who were outside of the chapel at the moment the child entered, the happiness expressed on every face, moved me so much that I could not keep from tears."

The child's nurse was named Madame Poitrine. "She is well named; for it is enormous, and the doctors say her milk is excellent. She is a genuine peasant woman, the wife of a gardener at Sceaux. She has a voice like a grenadier, swears with the greatest readiness; but that makes no difference, in fact, it is an advantage; for nothing surprises or disturbs her, so her milk is not affected. The laces and linen given to her did not surprise her. It seemed to her very simple; and she merely asked not to be compelled to put powder on her hair, because she had never used it; and she wanted to put on a cap worth six hundred francs over her hair, as she used to wear her mob-caps. Her voice amuses everybody, because she sometimes says very amusing things."

Every one admired the royal child; they even adored it. "I saw our little Dauphin this morning," Madame de Bombelles wrote again, October 29. "He is very well. He is as lovely as an angel; and the enthusiasm of the populace continues the same. In the streets one meets nothing but fiddles, and singing and dancing. I call that touching; and in fact, I know no more amiable nation than ours."

The general happiness spread over France, and even to foreign parts. Gustavus III., King of Sweden, wrote to the Count of Stedingk: "The details you sent to me about the delivery of the Queen of France gave me infinite pleasure. No one could take more interest in it than I do; and I assure you the joy at Drottningholm over the Dauphin's birth is as great as it can be at Versailles."

The different guilds went to pay their respects to the King and Queen. When they had entered the courtyard of the palace, headed by bands, they formed groups, as if they were on the stage. Chimney-sweeps carried a chimney, on the top of which they had fastened one of the smallest of their number. Chairmen carried a richly gilded chair with a nurse and child inside of it. Butchers appeared with a huge ox. Locksmiths were beating on an anvil. The cobblers had a little pair of boots for the Dauphin; the tailors, a suit of his regimental uniform. But alas! even at the happiest hours of Marie Antoinette's life there is no lack of black presentiments. There is a note of Shakespearian tragedy in her lot. Among the guilds there was a gravedigger's scene, in which they appeared with their tools; forgetting the gloomy nature of their duties, they wished to take part in the general rejoicing. But at the moment when they were passing along the terrace, Madame Sophie, the aunt of Louis XVI., had a shivering fit, and a few weeks later she was dead.

When the guilds had all passed by, fifty women from the Market, dressed in black, and nearly all wearing diamonds, were introduced into the Queen's room and had the honor of presenting their congratulations. Then came the turn of the fishwomen. "Sire," said one of them, "if Heaven owed a son to a king who regards his people as his family, our prayers and wishes had long demanded one. These are at length answered. We are sure that our children will be as happy as ourselves, for this child must be like you. You will teach him, Sire, to be good and just, like yourself. We take upon ourselves the duty of teaching our children how to love and respect their king." Then, turning to Marie Antoinette, the fishwoman said: "It is so long, Madame, that we have loved you without daring to say so, that we need all our respect in order not to abuse the permission to express it to you." Finally, turning to the cradle in which the Dauphin was lying, "You cannot understand the wishes which we utter over your cradle; but some day perhaps they will be told to you; they limit themselves to seeing in you the image of those who have given you life."

The locksmiths of Versailles accompanied their homage to the King with the present of a piece of their workmanship. It was a secret lock. Louis XVI., who took a great interest in mechanics, wanted to find out the secret for himself; he did so, and at the moment when he found out the combination, there sprang from the lock a steel dauphin of admirable workmanship. The King was delighted; he said that their present gave him great pleasure, and rewarded them handsomely.

January 21, 1782, the city of Paris gave great festivities to celebrate the birth of an heir to the throne. January 21! Always fateful dates! Always mysterious forebodings! What was to happen exactly eleven years later to a day? But why think of the terrible future? Let us drive away gloomy thoughts! Is it not right that Marie Antoinette, with such trials and tortures before her, should have her hour of glory and triumph? What grace and charm masked the beautiful and august Queen on that day when Providence seemed to bless her, and France was uttering one long cry of love, admiration, and devotion! What success! What applause! What ovations! How majestic she was when she appeared beneath the portal of Notre Dame, or when she ascended the grand staircase of the Hôtel de Ville! That evening, all Paris was illuminated; the Place Vendôme, the Place Louis XV., the Palais Bourbon, were ablaze with lights. The decorations of the Hôtel de Ville were magnificent with golden vessels filled with lilies, purple stuffs, columns, balustrades, and bands of music. The fireworks represented the Temple of Hymen. Before the door France was to be seen receiving from on high the august child just born.

Ah! let the Queen enjoy in peace these last moments of happiness! Let her still believe in the fidelity and kindness of her subjects! Let her still nourish the illusion that she rules over a loyal and chivalrous people! She is at the summit of her glory; but there are certain heights which cannot be reached without peril. In happiness, as in the atmosphere, there are certain limits which mortals may not pass. Whoever has been the object of enthusiastic praise and intoxicating flattery must await criticism and abuse. Kings and queens, geniuses and great artists, suffer this same fate. All happiness and glory must be paid for. Whoever you may be, if you are the idol of the multitude, tremble; unhappiness is not far off: after the palms, Calvary!

How false is joy! What is blinder than hope? This Dauphin, whose cradle is girt with such cries of love, so many blessings and songs, is to have a gloomy fate. His agony will coincide with that of the French Monarchy. A child, weak and doomed, like the royalty he represents, he will be plunged into sadness and overwhelmed with grief. His sufferings will plunge his mother into despair, and will throw a black veil over a period already so gloomy. He is to die at the moment when the States-General are opened, which were so fatal to the crown; and the public, in its revolutionary fervor, will pay but little attention to the death of this child, whose birth called forth such transports. The deputies of the Third Estate will have no respect for the tears of Louis XVI. They will want to talk business with him in the first hours of his mourning; and the unhappy father, wounded by this lack of tact and such indifference to the holiest feelings, will not be able to refrain from exclaiming with bitterness, "These gentlemen then have no children!"

II.

THE GRAND DUKE PAUL AT VERSAILLES.

BEFORE considering the calamities, it is pleasant to linger over the period of the last illusions — the time when, as the Count of Ségur said, the old social edifice was undermined, although there was no slightest sign of its approaching fall; when the change of manners was unperceived, because it had been gradual; when the court etiquette was the same, and one saw only the same throne, the same names, the same distinctions of rank, the same forms. The royal star, like a setting sun, still lit the horizon with magnificent brilliancy. France was more influential than ever. The Revolution was only lying latent; and the aristocracy, like a man smitten with mortal illness, but thinking himself in perfect health, was never fuller of charm, of elegance, of fire.

Let us glance at the court at a moment when, for an extraordinary occasion, it appeared in all its glory and in a sort of coquetry exhibited its full splendor. The richest uniforms, the costliest dresses, made their appearance; the most precious jewels issued from their cases. Louis XVI. himself desired pomp, and remembered that he was the heir of Louis XIV. Marie Antoinette was in full radiance.

The son and future successor of Catherine the Great, the Grand Duke Paul, who, travelling under the name of the Count du Nord, with his wife, Marie Fedorovna, Princess of Würtemberg, Montbéliard, had just reached France to visit Louis XVI. May 19, 1782, he went to Versailles *incognito* and heard mass, hiding in a tribune of the palace chapel, took part in a procession of Knights of the Holy Ghost, and returned to Paris in the evening, full of enthusiasm for the court, the dresses, the ceremonies, and especially for the Queen's beauty.

The next day the Grand Duke and the Grand Duchess, accompanied by the Russian Ambassador, Prince Bariatinsky, and all the members of the Embassy, made their formal entrance into Versailles. Louis XVI. was waiting for them in his large study (the bedchamber of Louis XIV.). "Sire," said the Grand Duke as he approached the King, "how happy I am to see Your Majesty! That was my main object in coming to France. My mother, the Empress, will envy me this happiness; for in that, as in all things, our feelings are the same."

Then the Grand Duke entered the Dauphin's apartment. He called him a very fine child, kissed him several times, and asked many questions of his governess, the Princess of Guéménée. "Madame," he said to her, "speak very often to the Dauphin of to-day's visit; remind him of the attachment I promise him in his cradle; let it be a pledge of a lasting alliance and union between our countries."

The same day there was a state dinner in the hall of the Grand Couvert, and after dinner a concert in the drawing-room of Peace. The palace was illuminated as on the days of levee. A thousand lights hung from the ceiling, and candelabra holding forty candles were set over each pier-table.

The Grand Duchess had brought with her to France a young lady belonging to the Alsatian nobility, the Baroness d'Oberkirch (who left the delightful Memoirs). Since she was not a Russian, she could not be presented either by the Grand Duchess or by the Russian Ambassador; but the Queen sent a footman to the Baroness to invite her to the concert, without the formality of a presentation. She said to the Grand Duchess, "I should have been very unkind if I had deprived you of your friend when I was anxious, on the other hand, to make everything pleasant for you." Then turning to Madame d'Oberkirch, she said: "You are very fortunate, Madame, to have so illustrious a friend; I really envy you, but I cannot help envying, too, the Countess du Nord the possession of such a friend as she says that you are." Marie Antoinette spoke to the Baroness d'Oberkirch five or six times during the concert. "You come from a region," she said to her, "which I found on my way here very beautiful and very loyal; I shall never forget that it was there I received the first greetings of the French. It was there that I was first called Queen."

Madame Campan tells us that Marie Antoinette, who did the honors of Versailles to her Russian guests with such amiable and attractive majesty, was very much frightened before she went into the room in which she was to dine with the illustrious travellers. She asked for a glass of water and said it was harder to play the part of a queen before other sovereigns and future monarchs than with her own courtiers. But she soon overcame her timidity, and was all grace and charm, inspiring every one with her brilliancy.

May 23, an opera was given in the great theatre of Versailles, "that hall which by its shape and the richness of its decorations and its gilding, looked like a fairy palace. The opera chosen was 'Aline; or, the Queen of Golconda,' which was taken from a short story of the Chevalier de Boufflers, to whom, it seems, something of the sort had really happened. The scenery was new and remarkably lifelike. One would gladly have been Aline, to rule over such a country."

June 6, Marie Antoinette gave a grand festival at the Little Trianon. In the theatre, a perfect gem, was played "Zémire and Azor," by Grétry. There was a display of diamonds which dazzled every eye; then after the opera, there was a supper, with three tables, and a hundred places at each one. The Grand Duchess wore on her head a little bird of precious stones, so brilliant that it was almost impossible to look at it; it was set to swinging while it beat its wings over a rose. That evening Madame d'Oberkirch was trying for the first time a little arrangement which was very fashionable, although tolerably uncomfortable. It consisted of little flat bottles, curved to follow the shape of the head, and containing a little water in which lay the ends of the flowers worn in the hair, thus retaining their freshness. "That device," she said, "did not always succeed, but when it did, it was charming. This look of spring on the head, amid powdered snow, was most striking." After supper, they all walked in the gardens. Fireworks lent a magic glow to the trees, the plants, and the lake. The green glass-plots became red, blue, and yellow in turn. A lantern was hung in every shrub. A perfect summer night gave charm and poetry to the entertainment. The illuminations on the earth rivalled with the moon and stars above. A band of music hidden in the greenery filled the enchanted garden with sweet sounds. Marie Antoinette, in all her splendor, appeared like a goddess.

June 8, there was a ball at Versailles in the Gallery of the Mirrors. This gallery, which is seventy-three metres long, ten metres and forty centimetres broad, and thirteen metres high, with its full arch vault decorated throughout by Lebrun, with its seventeen arched windows opposite which were arches all filled with mirrors, made a wonderful place for a ball. There were abundant chandeliers, and candelabra, and lamps. The King made his entrance from the drawing-room of War, the Queen hers from that of Peace. On these occasions, nobles and ladies made it a point of honor to appear in as grand dress as possible. The French nobility moved to and fro in a most brilliant procession, and the foreigners who were present were amazed at its incomparable splendor.

At the ball of June 8, the Grand Duke uttered one of those happy phrases which won for him much reputation during his stay in France. Louis XVI., who was surrounded by a throng of courtiers, among whom was the Russian prince, complained of being incommoded by the crowd. Then, when every one was intimidated by this remark of the King's, the Grand Duke said, " Sire, excuse me; I have become so thoroughly a Frenchman, that like them I thought I could not get too near Your Majesty." He danced with the Queen. Marie Antoinette, who was then in the full flower of her beauty, had never been more gracious or more imposing. In the course of the ball she said to the Baroness d'Oberkirch, with her customary kindliness: " Speak a little German to me, that I may find out if I still remember it. Now I only know the language of my new country." The Baroness spoke a few words of German; the Queen pondered for a few seconds, and then went on, " Ah! I am delighted to hear German again; you speak it, Madame, like a Saxon, with no Alsatian accent, which surprises me. German is a fine language; but French, it seems to me, when I hear my children speaking, the sweetest language in the world!"

June 9, there was a grand review of the French Guards, at the Champ de Mars, in honor of the Grand Duke. The aged Marshal de Biron marched at the head of this fine regiment, which was always a favorite of the city. The Parisians, who always delighted in military displays, were beside themselves with joy, and full of delight and admiration of the French and Russian uniforms. They drank, sang, and danced as if they were at the Porcherons. There was no limit to the applause and merry-making.

The next day the Grand Duke and the Grand Duchess went to Chantilly, where the Prince of Condé gave them a magnificent reception. "Chantilly," says Madame d'Oberkirch, "is the most beautiful place in the world. The lakes, the woods, the gardens, are delightful; the naïads at the fountains have quite the air of the court, and the sandy roads in the forest are a thousand times more charming than those of a flower-garden. The princes of the House of Condé have always been grand and chivalrous, and, too, I know not exactly why, they have always been more popular with the nobility than their elders, the Princes of Orleans. The Prince of Condé and the Duke of Bourbon have a large suite of gentlemen, all famous for bravery and loyalty. The intimates of the Palais Royal, on the other hand, are held in slight esteem and honor, and are not received anywhere else. They are evil company for a young man; they are a bad sign. The Count du Nord made some just and profound remarks on the subject; he said, speaking of the Duke of Chartres: 'The King of France is very tolerant! If my mother had a cousin like him, he would not stay long in Russia.'"

Revolutionary ideas were beginning to get a foothold at the Palais Royal, while Chantilly was a sort of sanctuary of the monarchical faith. The Grand Duke Paul was much pleased with this charming residence, when the Prince of Condé, a model of courtesy, received him in great pomp. There were two dinners at the castle; the table was covered with an inexhaustible supply of gold and silver plate. After each course, the servants, without noise or confusion, threw all these magnificent vessels out of the window. But nothing was lost: precious vessels, jugs, and dishes fell into the water of the moats, whence they were taken out in large nets. At the play, the back of the stage opened, disclosing the wood, fields, fountains, and lawn, where Vestris, as *Zéphir*, was dancing on the grass. In the evening, supper was served in the hamlet, a collection of huts like those on the stage of the opera, in the middle of an English garden. They passed through the Isle of Love, exactly like one of Watteau's pictures; there was a statue there of a cupid holding a burning heart. On the pedestal was carved this inscription, which is thoroughly in the taste of the time: —

"Offering but a heart to Beauty,
As naked as Truth;
Unarmed, like Innocence;

Wingless, like Constancy, —
Such was Love in the Golden Age:
We find him not, but we still seek him."

A pavilion had been constructed in the grove, and on the top was placed a band, which could not be seen below, and the music seemed to come from the skies.

Mademoiselle de Condé, who was then twenty-five years old, who had been but two years out of the convent, and was soon to take the veil, helped her father to do the honors at Chantilly to the illustrious foreigners. She was a very intelligent woman, of great beauty, and as worthy as she was beautiful. She had every gift and talent; she sang, played the harpsichord, painted, and composed poetry. The Grand Duchess said that, next to the Queen, the woman who best pleased her at court, the woman whom she would have wanted for a friend, was Mademoiselle de Condé. On leaving, the Russian Princess was presented with a bouquet by a pretty boy: this boy was the Duke of Enghien, later the victim of Vincennes.

The festivities at Chantilly made a great deal of talk, for there had been a greater show of the luxury and magnificence of the old régime than even at Versailles. The Parisians said: "The King received the Count du Nord like a friend; the Duke of Orleans, like a private citizen; the Prince of Condé, like a sovereign."

The son of the great Catherine had much success

in France, where all the wise heads perceived the advantages of an alliance with Russia. Grimm said, speaking of the Grand Duke: "At Versailles he seemed to know the court of France as well as his own. In the artists' studios, especially in those of Greuze and Houdin, he showed great familiarity with art, and expressed intelligent admiration. In our schools and academies he made it clear by his praise and questions that there was no form of talent or of work which did not interest him, and that he had long known all the men whose abilities or virtues had honored their time and their country. His conversation, and all his remarks which have been repeated, announce not merely a delicate and cultivated intelligence, but also an exquisite feeling for the finest points of our language."

The Grand Duke and the Grand Duchess left Versailles June 19, 1782, to return to Russia. As they were leaving, the Chevalier du Coudray addressed them in these lines: —

> "By your agreeable presence
> You have fulfilled all our wishes.
> By your departure, your absence,
> Princes, you arouse our keenest regrets.
> Such are now the farewells of France!
> You ought to stay, or you ought never to have come."

III.

"THE MARRIAGE OF FIGARO."

DURING the stay of the Grand Duke Paul in France, Beaumarchais had done his best to interest the Russian prince in the lot of the "Marriage of Figaro." This play, which had been written six or seven years before, was famous before it was acted, and in spite of his untiring efforts, the author, skilful as he was, could not get permission to have it played. Against him he had the King, the magistrates, the Lieutenant of Police, Keeper of the Seals. Louis XVI., after reading the manuscript, had said: "It is detestable. The Bastille would have to be destroyed to prevent dangerous consequences from the performance of such a play. This man turns to ridicule everything which should be respected in a government." "Then it won't be played?" asked Marie Antoinette. "No, of course not," answered the King; "you may be sure of that."

Well, even after this statement of the King's had become known there were many willing to bet that the play would nevertheless be acted, so thoroughly known were the fickleness and feebleness of the authorities. Beaumarchais had said in the piece that only little men were afraid of little writings. Many great lords, who were averse to passing for little men, felt obliged ardently to defend the " Marriage of Figaro." The Baron de Breteuil and all the members of the society of the Polignacs were among the warmest defenders of the play. The manuscript was handed about in high society, and the most distinguished people touched with reverence the pages fastened with pink ribbons. The privilege of reading the " Marriage " was much sought after by fashionable people, and those who were fortunate enough to have read it were much envied.

The Grand Duke Paul was one of this number; he thought the play very amusing, and Catherine II. offered to have it brought out in Russia. But Beaumarchais, whose course has been so well described by M. de Loménie in his excellent book, " Beaumarchais et son temps," in spite of all his zeal and the influence of his friends, could not secure the removal of the prohibition which forbade its performance. June 12, 1783, he came very near succeeding by surprise. By means of a tacit sufferance, due to the protection of the Count of Artois, he had been able to order a rehearsal of the play at the theatre of Menues Plaisirs; that is to say, in the King's own theatre. Tickets had been distributed bearing a picture of Figaro in his dress of an Andalusian barber. The carriages were beginning to arrive.

The Count of Artois was on his way from Versailles to Paris, to see this long and impatiently awaited rehearsal, when the Duke of Villequier came to tell him that it would not take place, that the King had forbidden it. It has been asserted that Beaumarchais exclaimed in an outburst of wrath: "Well, gentlemen, my play can't be acted here, it seems, and I take my oath that it shall be played — perhaps in the very choir of Notre Dame." This prophecy was not to be fulfilled to the letter, but the end of the eighteenth century was to see something still more scandalous in the choir of Notre Dame, — a prostitute enthroned upon the high altar, and receiving adoration as the Goddess of Reason.

Beaumarchais, this forerunner of the Revolution, this man of intrigues and strife, this many-sided creature, — watchmaker, musician, ship-owner, financier, pleader, comic author, — this immoral moralist, in spite of his pretence of regenerating the world, this bold publicist, distinctly modern in his loud ways and his fondness for advertising himself, was he not the type of the new society? An intelligent observer might have understood that the jingle of the fool's bells would soon be followed by the sound of the tocsin, and before long the Figaros of the time would change their satin and velvet jackets for the carmagnole.

But society, in its giddiness and thoughtlessness, cared only for pleasure. Confident, joyous, full of life, fancying itself strong and renewed, it regarded serious men as pedants and liked to see itself laughed at. To amuse itself at its own expense, to hiss its image on the stage, seemed a charming idea! Were not the noblemen of the time of Louis XVI. like the flagellants of the court of Henri III., who flogged themselves as they walked in processions? The deeper their scars, the greater their happiness. What awaited the old régime was not illness, but suicide; a merry suicide, accompanied with jest and song, preceded by witty speeches, biting epigrams, and suppers in which abundant champagne should flow.

Nothing amused the nobles like a satire on nobility. The more they lived on privileges, the louder they denounced abuses. Voltaire had admirers among the clergy. Beaumarchais himself, with all his marvellous intelligence, had no idea of the full significance of his attacks or of the importance of his play, which was not an amusement, but an event. He no more desired the fall of the throne than the overthrow of the altar. At heart he was a monarchist, and he would not have been pleased to see his Figaro turn republican. Cold water and black bread had no charms for him, and he was one of those who, tyrants for tyrants, preferred the red heels to the red caps. He did not have the tastes of a demagogue; possibly he wrote revolutionary literature, as M. Jourdain spoke prose, without knowing it.

Nevertheless, lords and ladies were intriguing to have the play brought out. September 26, 1783, one of the leaders of the society of the Little Trianon, a friend of the Duchess of Polignac, the Count de Vaudreuil, succeeded in having it played at his castle of Gennevilliers, before three hundred persons, by the actors of the Comédie Française. The Count of Artois and the Duchess of Polignac were among the spectators. If we may trust Madame Vigée-Lebrun, Beaumarchais was beside himself: "When some one complained of the heat, he did not wait to have the windows opened, but thrust his stick through the panes, so that after the play it was said that he had hit out in two ways."

The amiable Louis XVI. let himself be carried away by the general enthusiasm. He was assured that the play had been much cut; that it was no longer dangerous, and at last consented to its performance. He imagined that it would have no success, but he was sadly mistaken; never did a comedy enjoy such a triumph.

The first performance was in Paris, April 27, 1784, in the theatre of the Comédie Française, now the Odéon. There was the wildest struggle for tickets. Nobles applied for a place in the *claque*. Grandees awaited their turn in the long line. Women of the highest rank took their place, in the early morning, in the actresses' boxes, breakfasting and dining there, putting themselves under their protection, in the hope of entering among the first. The guards were swept aside, the doors burst open, the barriers torn down, people smothered; nothing was lacking to the author's glory. He had just been dining with an amiable priest, the Abbé de Calonne, a brother of the minister, whom he had invited by this note: —

"Come! come! My Andalusian barber cannot celebrate his marriage without your official bond. Like sovereigns, he will invite by placards twelve thousand persons to his nuptials. Will they be happy? I do not know. This child was conceived in joy. I hope he may be born without suffering. I already feel the first pains, and I have had a wretched time hitherto. I shall need consolation and very spiritual aid at the moment of the crisis. I expect them from you and from another priest (the Abbé Sabathier) in a very dark corner. *Venite, abbati, maledicemus de auctore;* but above all, let us laugh at my griefs: that is all I ask. I salute you, honor you, and love you."

In a narrow, close box, between the two priests, Beaumarchais examined the audience with great satisfaction. More than one duchess, as Grimm said, would have been glad to find in the galleries, where ladies never went, a little footstool, by the side of Mesdames Duthé, Carlin, etc. The playhouse was most brilliantly lit by a new method; the audience was noisy and well disposed. When the naval hero, the Bailiff de Suffren, entered, there was a round of applause, and another, a moment later, when the charming actress, Madame Dugazon, appeared.

The performance began at half-past five, and was not over till ten. At that time a play that lasted four and a half hours was something unheard of.

Contrary to the usual custom, there was no short play before the long one. Was not the "Marriage of Figaro" enough to satisfy the general curiosity? Its success was enormous. As La Harpe has said, "It is easy to conceive of the joy and delight of the public which found a charm in amusing itself at the expense of the authorities, and consented to be ridiculed on the stage." Sainte-Beuve has said, "The old society would not have so well deserved its fate, if it had not been there that evening, and a hundred successive evenings, in raptures over the merry, wild, indecent, insolent mockery of itself, and if it had not taken so grand a part in its own mystification." Beaumarchais himself said, "There is something more amazing than my play; that is, its success."

The actors and actresses outdid themselves. Every word told; every bit of satire was received with continual applause. The public recognized itself in this picture of Figaro: "Never out of temper, always in good humor, devoting the present to joy, and caring as little for the future as for the past, lively, generous! generous —"

"As a thief!" says Bartholo. "As a lord," says Marceline.

There was great delight among the audience at this definition of a courtier: —

"*Figaro.* I was born to be a courtier.
"*Suzanne.* I am told it is a difficult profession.
"*Figaro.* Receive, take, and ask; there's the secret in three words."

This reflection, which was also a just one, was received with laughter: —

"*The Count.* The servants in this house take longer to dress than their masters."
"*Figaro.* It's because they have no valets to help them."

Here is an intelligent remark on the chances an official has for promotion: —

"*The Count.* With character and intelligence, you may some day rise in the office.
"*Figaro.* Intelligence a help to advancement? your lordship is laughing at mine. Be commonplace and cringing, and one can get anywhere."

And after this keen remark is a picture of diplomacy drawn by the clear-sighted barber: "To pretend to be ignorant of what every one knows, and to know what every one else does not know, to understand what nobody comprehends, not to hear what every one hears, and, above all, to be able to do the impossible; often to have for the secret one must hide the fact that there is none; to lock one's self up to cut quills, and to seem deep when one is only, as they say, empty and hollow; to play a part ill or well, to set spies and pension traitors; to loosen seals, intercept letters, and try to dignify the meanness of the methods by the importance of the objects, — that's politics, or I'm a dead man."

The diplomatists who were in the audience laughed heartily at this description of their occupation. The great ladies were delighted at the truth of this remark of Suzanne's to the Countess: "I have noticed how much the habits of society enable ladies to tell lies without showing it." They warmly applauded this democratic, but very true, remark of the same Suzanne: "Do women of my station have vapours? It is a malady of fashionable people, and prevails only in boudoirs." The lords, who were always surrounded with fawning parasites, applauded with enthusiasm Figaro's remark to Basil: "Are you a prince to be flattered? Hear the truth, you wretch, since you have not money to recompense a liar." But the moment when the enthusiasm turned to delirium, to frenzy, when dukes and peers, ministers, Knights of Saint Louis, and Knights of the Holy Ghost, were transported to the seventh heaven, was when the bold barber, suddenly turning into a tribune, said to them all: "Because you are a great lord, you fancy yourself a great genius! Nobility, wealth, rank, office, — all that makes you very proud! What have you done for all these blessings? You have taken the trouble to be born, and nothing else!"

The officials in charge of the censorship were particularly delighted with this sentence in the same monologue: "Provided I don't speak in my writings of authority, of religion, of politics, of morality, of the officials, of influential bodies, of other spectacles, of any one who has any claim to anything, I can print anything freely, under the inspection of two or three censors."

The ministers in charge of public duties found

much justice in this phrase: "I was thought of for a place, but unfortunately I was suited for it: they needed an accountant; it was a dancer who got it." Those in whose drawing-rooms gaming went on felt obliged to applaud this: "There was nothing left for me to do, except steal; I made myself banker at a faro table; since then, good people, I sup out, and people who are called *comme il faut* open their houses to me very politely, reserving to themselves three-quarters of the profits."

Napoleon I. said of Beaumarchais's comedy that it was the Revolution already in action. This Figaro, who said "he had seen everything, done everything, dared everything," who declared that "for success, tact was better than knowledge"; this unscrupulous barber, who "left smoke for fools to fatten on, and shame on the roadside, because it is too heavy a load for pedestrians to carry"; this being, "plying every trade to get a livelihood, here a master, there a valet, as fortune directs; ambitious from vanity, hardworking by necessity, but idle — with delight; an orator in danger, a poet for amusement, a musician on occasion, in love by fits and starts"; this man to whom Suzanne, who knows him well, says, "Intrigue and money, you are in your proper sphere," — this Figaro already talks like a member of the clubs. Jests are not enough for him; he requires long speeches; he makes advances to the pit. The Revolution is not remote.

Is the "Marriage of Figaro" a school of morality?

Not the least in the world. Basil, that singular parody of the Spanish priest, "that pedant of oratorio," as Figaro calls him, has very advanced theories about conjugal fidelity. "Is wishing well to a woman, wishing ill to her husband? . . . Of all the serious things in the world, marriage is the absurdest." Count Almaviva thinks that "love is the romance of the heart; pleasure is its history." Does the play end with a making over of morals? Not in the least. The upshot is that Figaro, become rich, and married to a pretty wife, will never lack friends. "I was poor," he says, "and I was despised. I showed some wit, and I was hated. A pretty wife and a fortune" — and Bartholo shouts out, "Every heart will turn to you!" As to the populace, it will continue to suffer and to sing, as Brid'oison declares in the first lines: —

> "Now, gentlemen, this comedy,
> Which you judge at this moment,
> Saving error, paints the life
> Of the good people who hear it.
> When they are oppressed, they curse and cry
> And agitate themselves in every way:
> All ends in songs."

Almaviva is the old régime; Figaro, the new society. Almaviva is corrupt. He regards adultery as a very simple, natural thing — on the part of the husband, that is. But he is always in good form. Even when angry he is a man of good society. Doubtless his faults are great; he is "a libertine from idleness, jealous through vanity," yet he is not odious — what do I say? he is not ridiculous. Derided in the last imbroglio, he yet plays a better part than Figaro, who believes that he is a deceived husband before the nuptial blessing, and yet, instead of suffering from it, finds time for his peroration and the utterance of maxims. Almaviva will never correct himself. He will still run after Suzanne, but he will never betray his king.

As for Figaro, with his double passion for intrigue and for gold, what will become of him? In summing up I am tempted to say, with a man who cannot be suspected of partiality for the old régime, — with Sainte-Beuve: "If we take the two characters as types of two contrasted societies, there is room for hesitation, if we are honest men, and we may prefer, after all, to live in a society under the rule of Almavivas, than in one which Figaros should govern. . . . Figaro is a sort of professor, who gives systematic instructions, — I will not say to the middle classes, but to upstarts and pretenders of every class, — in insolence." However, neither the Count nor the barber is estimable, and Beaumarchais, who had but a faint belief in human virtue, did not paint with glowing colors either the past or the future, either the old régime or the new.

IV.

GUSTAVUS III. AT VERSAILLES.

JUNE 7, 1784, Gustavus III., who was on his way back from Italy, travelling incognito as the Count of Haga, reached Paris; he took up his quarters in the rue du Bac, at the house of his ambassador, the Baron de Staël, and the same evening he went to Versailles without announcing his visit. Louis XVI. was hunting at Rambouillet; but when he received word from a courtier sent by M. de Vergennes, he left his brother to sup with the hunters and left at once for Versailles. There he dressed quickly and appeared before his guest with one red-heeled and one black-heeled shoe, a gold buckle and a silver buckle. The meeting of the two monarchs was most cordial. A magnificent apartment in the palace was made ready for the King of Sweden; but he, desiring greater liberty, declined the invitation to stay there, and took lodgings in the town.

At that time the Swedes were called the French of the north, and the relations between the courts of Versailles and Stockholm were very close. Gustavus III. was very popular in France, where he had already been, in the reign of Louis XV. The Liberals were very glad to pardon him his coup d'état in 1772, and the philosophers looked upon him as one of their followers. The most fashionable ladies loved and admired him; he used to write to them regularly. He was well educated, witty, generous, fond of luxury, the fine arts, and pleasure, and there was about him something very sympathetic, original, and attractive.

In 1784, as during his first visit, all classes of French society gave him the warmest welcome. At the theatre he was cheered; and if he arrived after the piece was begun, the actors would go back and commence it anew. At the supper-tables of the Countesses of Boufflers and La Marck, of the Duchess of La Vallière, of the Princesses of Lamballe and Croy, at the Richelieu and d'Aiguillon mansions, he was received with the subtlest flattery and the most delicate homage.

Never had the court and the town been more attractive. Marie Antoinette was in the flower of her beauty and her charm; the year before Louis XVI. had signed a glorious peace which established the independence of the United States, banished the memories of the Seven Years' War, gave credit to the arms and diplomacy of France, and showed its honest and venerable King in the light of a moderate, powerful, peace-loving monarch, an arbiter between two worlds, a protector of liberty for many races. Calonne's financial schemes inspired confidence in inexhaustible wealth and resources. A loan that had been skilfully placed gave everything an appearance of marvellous prosperity.

All the Memoirs of the time bear witness to the security, the confidence, the satisfied national pride, the content, enjoyed by France in this year 1784, when money was abundant, the crops were most rich, optimism was the order of the day, and of all the people in the world, the French seemed the most devoted to their sovereigns and the easiest to govern. Life and hope were full of promise; a cultivated society, tolerant, animated with new ideas, was in the enjoyment of liberty, abundance, and pleasure. It was a delightful epoch, refined, sentimental, witty, when no one believed in the power of evil, and every one hoped, through science and philosophy, to overthrow ignorance and suffering; when intellectual pleasures were triumphant and every audacious thought dared to assert itself! "Adversity," says the Count of Ségur in his Memoirs, "is harsh, suspicious, and gloomy; happiness inspires tolerance and confidence. Hence in this period of prosperity there was a free scope for plans of reformation, for every proposed innovation, for the most liberal thoughts, for the boldest schemes." The government did not want to make itself feared; its sole ambition was to make itself loved.

French society was then regarded by all Europe as the highest type of wit and politeness. France, by its ideas, its literature, its luxury, set the fashion for the world; and foreign princes visited it to pay homage to a superior civilization. Never had Paris been so popular. New quarters had been devoted to amusements of all sorts; the Palais Royal, with its many shops and extreme animation, was laying the foundations of its fame; the boulevards, which had been recently laid out and planted with trees, were filling up with rich dwellings, coffee-houses, and theatres. Gustavus III. delighted to mingle, unrecognized, with the crowd of Parisian idlers. Later, towards the end of his life, when harassed by perpetual conspiracies and by a war in Finland against the Russians, he was to be homesick for Paris; and he was heard to say that he wanted to abdicate, in order to return thither to live on the boulevards.

"We live in an age of wonders," exclaimed Bachaumont, in an outburst of enthusiasm. "We were proud to be Frenchmen," said the Count of Ségur, "and prouder still to be Frenchmen of the eighteenth century, which we regarded as the Golden Age restored to earth by the new philosophy." The fashionable dogma was the unlimited perfectibility of man. No more war! was the general cry. No more tyranny! No more injustice! No more custom-houses! No more prejudices, or obstacles, or errors! Civilized man, reformed and purified! Society freed! Humanity triumphant! The glorious and peaceful reign of virtue, justice, and liberty! What might not be expected from a country that had produced men like Buffon, Lavoisier, and Montgolfier! What was to be the future of those occult sciences which already were filling the public with enthusiasm, — such as mesmerism, somnambulism, and magnetism? Even Gustavus III., who all his life was curious about the supernatural, tried Mesmer's magnetic tub, which so fired the imagination of the Parisians, and, as they believed, was destined to cure every ill. No longer could it be said that there is nothing new under the sun. The novelties of science became most startling. The year before, the first balloons had risen to the clouds; and no one doubted that navies would ride the air as they rode the ocean. Fouquet's motto, "Where shall I not ascend?" (*Quo non ascendam?*) no longer seemed fantastic. Man, who had conquered creation, was destined to control the elements.

June 23, 1784, a fire-balloon was sent up at Versailles, in the Minister's courtyard, before the palace, in the presence of the King of Sweden. It was decorated with the initials of Louis XVI. and Gustavus III., and with a white brassart, in memory of the coup d'état of 1772.

The Swedish King made a pilgrimage to Ermenonville, and in that little temple of philosophy paid a somewhat interested homage to the memory of the author of the "Social Contract" and the *La Nouvelle Héloïse*. The admirers of Jean Jacques Rousseau announced themselves the admirers of Gustavus III.

Marie Antoinette entertained the King of Sweden at the Little Trianon, and there, surrounded by the young Swedish officers whom the court of Versailles received most kindly, he might have thought himself in his own country. Never had Marie Antoinette been more amiable and more charming. Marmontel and Grétry's "Awakened Sleeper" was acted with fine scenery and brilliant ballets. After the play in the delightful little theatre, supper was served in the English garden, under the trees, which were illuminated by colored lanterns and fireworks. The Queen would not take a seat at the table, being anxious to do all the honors to her guests. All the ladies were dressed in white. It was, as Gustavus himself said, a real scene from fairyland, a sight worthy of the Elysian Fields.

At the same time the King wrote the following letter to Louis XVI.: "Two friends ought to talk over their common interests with perfect frankness, and when two kings, like ourselves, are personally acquainted, it behooves our dignity that we treat with each other directly. . . . Having been educated since my tenderest infancy in a firm friendship for France, and having been strengthened in this feeling by that of the late King, Louis XV., which he manifested in the most perilous moments of my life, my most constant aim has been to testify to him, as also to Your Majesty, my sincere gratitude and my desire to perpetuate the union which has so long existed between our two countries."

The journey of Gustavus III. proves the high position then held by France in the eyes of foreign nations. If the Revolution had not broken out in France, its diplomacy would have brought forth important results, and its system of alliances would have become most firmly fixed. Louis XVI., who was the object of universal esteem and respect, interested himself most carefully and intelligently in foreign affairs. He played a very important part in the European concert, and his ambassadors were superior men, who represented him most worthily in foreign countries. With their enlightenment, their courage, their general aptitude, their historical traditions, and the examples of their great men, the wonderful climate, its zone of waves and mountains, what power might not the French have attained, if they had not been divided against themselves?

July 19, 1784, Gustavus III. signed with Louis XVI. a favorable treaty of alliance. The next day he left for Sweden, well content with the results of his journey, delighted with the French court, with no suspicion of the tragic lot in reserve for his host and for himself.

It seems that all the figures who appeared, even for a moment, on the scene at Versailles, were condemned by an inexorable fatality. We might say that every one who crossed the threshold of this palace was thereby doomed in advance to exile, captivity, or death. The conspirators' pistols, the strangler's bowstring, the headsman's axe, were hidden in the dark mystery of the future. The smell of blood was already mingling with the perfumes of the court. The hour was approaching when the Grand Duke Paul of Russia and Gustavus III. of Sweden, the two princes who had been so graciously received in France, were to be surrounded by assassins.

Gustavus, the king so admired by philosophers, became, in his later years, the victim of absurd superstitions and credulity which is the punishment at all times of the lack of faith. Long before he fell beneath the blows of traitors, he felt that he was in the toils of a hidden conspiracy. He tried to distract himself in the tumult of noisy pleasures, which he crowded one upon another, but everywhere and always the dark presentiment pursued him. At last, in the fine theatre of Stockholm, where his love of the stage had produced many marvels, he was struck down at a court ball, at which he appeared in a domino, by regicide courtiers.

Paul I., a crowned Hamlet, desired to avenge his father. A martyr to his greatness, he suffered on his throne, at the height of his power, inexpressible anguish and grief. This generous man, this great Russian patriot, full of the national genius, a human, intelligent, lovable prince, whom Paris and Versailles had so justly and warmly greeted, was to be treated as a madman, and, like Gustavus III., to be assassinated by his own courtiers.

V.

"THE BARBER OF SEVILLE" AT THE TRIANON.

IT was the month of August, 1785; Marie Antoinette, who had been installed since the 3d in her favorite summer residence, the Little Trianon, was to stay there till the 24th, the day before the festival of Saint Louis. "This outing," says Metra, "is an almost continual ball. The lords and ladies of the court dance beneath a large tent. The different persons of Versailles are admitted, and the parties are many and gay." There was nothing prettier or more rural than the Sunday balls on the lawns of the Little Trianon. The Queen, in her white linen dress, set aside the sceptre for the shepherd's crook; royalty became a pastoral like those of Florian. Lancret and Watteau no longer were the models; it was Greuze who set the fashion. At these Sunday balls every one who was properly dressed was admitted, especially nurses with young children. "Marie Antoinette," we read in the Memoirs of the Count of Vaublanc, "used to dance a square dance, to show that she took a part in the pleasures to which she had invited others. She used to summon the nurses, have the children presented to her, speak to them of their parents, and load them with attentions."

The charming entertainments were truly democratic. "I noticed, with one of my friends," continues the Count of Vaublanc, an eye-witness, "that very few who belonged to the highest society took part in these entertainments. They did not hold themselves aloof from haughtiness, for they every day were wearing plainer clothes, and it was more and more becoming the fashion not to wear one's orders; but rather from a delicacy about taking places which others passionately desired."

Marie Antoinette did not content herself with country balls; she was going to act plays. The theatre of the Little Trianon was made ready,—a real jewel, a work of art. At the present time it is closed to the public; a great pity, for it is so dainty, so charming, so replete with pleasant memories! Why hide such a gem in its case?

At the end of the flower-garden, on one of the sides of the French garden, near the summer-house which used to be the summer dining-room of Louis XV., are two Ionic columns, supporting a pediment, on which is a cupid holding a lyre and laurel wreath; that is the door of the theatre. The hall is in white and gold; the ceiling represents an Olympus, painted by Lagrenée. Above the curtain two nymphs support the coat-of-arms of the deity of the place, Marie Antoinette. The accommodations for the audience are small, but the stage is large enough for the most complicated plays. August 1, 1780, began the performances of the royal company. Grimm wrote at that time, in his *Correspondence:* "No one has ever seen, and no one will ever see, 'Le Roi et le Fermier,' or 'La Gageure imprévue,' played by more illustrious actors, or before a more imposing and more select audience. The Queen, who is endowed with every grace, and knows how to assume all without losing her own, played Jenny in the first piece, and took the soubrette's part in the second. All the other parts were taken by the intimate friends of Their Majesties and the royal family. The Count of Artois appeared as a game-keeper in the first play, and as a valet in the second. The Count of Vaudreuil, perhaps the best amateur actor in Paris, took the part of Richard; the Duchess of Guiche (the daughter of the Duchess of Polignac), of whom Horace might well have said, *Matre pulchrâ filia pulchrior*, that of the little Betzi; the Countess Diana of Polignac, that of the mother; and the Count of Adhémar, that of the king."

Marie Antoinette was fond of the emotions of the stage. And is there not a resemblance between real queens and theatre queens? They are equally in sight, and alike exposed to praise and blame.

September 19, 1780, the illustrious actress, in her theatre at the Little Trianon, took, with great success, the part of Colette, in the "Devin du Village" of Jean Jacques Rousseau. She was very charming in this play. Her mother, the Empress Maria Theresa, did not approve of private theatricals, "knowing many instances," she wrote to the Count of Mercy-Argenteau, "in which these performances ended in some love affair, or scandal of some sort." The ambassador, who, in his letters to his sovereign, was a harsh judge of Marie Antoinette's amusements, was not bold enough to condemn severely the performance of the "Devin du Village," because he had received the distinguished favor of a special invitation to see it, incognito, from a closed box. Among the audience the sole members of the court were Monsieur, the King's brother, the Countess of Artois, and Madame Elisabeth. The boxes and balconies were filled by subordinate attendants. Not a single great lord, not a single fine lady, was admitted; there were no ministers, no diplomatists. The exception made in favor of the Austrian Ambassador was a very flattering one. Consequently, in his " very humble report" of October 24, 1780, he was more lenient than usual. "The Queen," he wrote, "has a very agreeable and harmonious voice; her way of acting is dignified and full of grace; in a word, the play was given as well as was possible for private theatricals. I noticed that the King watched it with manifest attention and pleasure. During the entr'actes he went on the stage and into the Queen's dressing-room."

It has been said that Louis XVI. hissed Marie Antoinette; also that the Queen, having summoned the guards, said to them at the end of the evening, advancing to the footlights: "Gentlemen, I have done my best to amuse you; I should have liked to act better, to give you more pleasure." The anecdotes are inexact; nothing of the sort happened.

These performances, which were interrupted by the death of Maria Theresa and the delicate condition of Marie Antoinette, were resumed in the summer of 1782 and 1783. The Queen supervised the minutest details of her little theatre, — scenery, machinery, costumes, setting, — she regulated everything. Her greatest success was as Babet in the "Matinée et la veillée villageoise," an operetta by Dezide. Babet, a village Cinderella lost her wooden shoe, like the fairy's slipper. Alas! what Marie Antoinette was to lose, was not a wooden shoe, or a slipper, but her crown.

In 1785 there was but one performance, and that was the last of all. Beaumarchais was then all the rage. The "Marriage of Figaro" had been given again most successfully, at the Théâtre Français, and the Queen, who had protected the author, conceived the idea of paying him the most unexpected honor, of giving in the Little Trianon the "Barber of Seville." "Imagine the pretty little pet, gentle, tender, easy, fresh, tempting, with her pretty foot, her slim waist, her trim figure, her plump arms, her pink lips, and her hands! her cheeks! her teeth! her eyes!" (The "Barber of Seville," Act II., Scene 2). Yes, this part of Rosina, this charming girl, this fascinating creature whom Figaro thus describes, was to be played by the most imposing and majestic of women, the Queen of France and of Navarre.

The rehearsals began under the direction of one of the best actors of the Comédie Française, Dazincourt, who had just made a great hit in the "Marriage of Figaro." It was during these preparations that the first rumors of the affair of the necklace reached the Queen. Marie Antoinette had summoned Madame Campan to the Little Trianon, and was rehearsing the part of Rosina with her when she heard from her of the horrible drama and the inconceivable enigma which was soon to fire all France with curiosity and wrath.

It was like a thunderbolt. The Queen perceived at a glance into what an abyss of calumny and disgrace her cowardly enemies were trying to hurl her. But she did not lose heart. She saw that to abandon the play, which had been announced, would be to confess her guilt and show her alarm. Far from countermanding the play, she continued to direct the preparations without a pause. August 15, 1785, the festival of the Assumption, the Cardinal de Rohan, Grand Almoner of France, was arrested, in his pontifical robes, just as he was about to ascend to the altar in the chapel of the palace of Versailles. Four days later, Marie Antoinette played Rosina in the "Barber of Seville."

Beaumarchais was present. The part of Figaro was taken by the Count of Artois; that of Almaviva, by the Count of Vaudreuil; Bartholo, by the Duke of Guiche; Bazile, by M. de Crussol. "The few spectators admitted to this performance," writes

Grimm in his *Correspondence*, "found in it a unity and harmony which are very rare in plays acted by amateurs. It was especially noticed that the Queen threw into the scene in the fourth act a grace and truth which would have won the most enthusiastic applause for even a less illustrious actress."

It was indeed a singular evening! At the very moment when so many catastrophes were preparing and so many storms gathering, it was odd to hear the brother of Louis XVI., the Count of Artois, exclaiming, in Figaro's Andalusian dress: "Upon my word, sir, since men have no other choice than between stupidity and madness, if I can't get any profit, I want at least pleasure; so, hurrah for happiness! Who knows if the world is going to last three weeks?" It was the sturdy upholder of the old régime, the future émigré, the prince who was to be known later as Charles X., who uttered democratic phrases like these: "I find myself very happy to be forgotten, being sure that a great man does us enough good when he does us no harm. As to the virtues which one requires in a servant, does Your Excellency know many masters who are worthy of being valets?" In this gaiety was there not more show than sincerity, something forced, something factitious, and was there not a forewarning in this speech of Figaro's in the mouth of the brother of Louis XVI.: "I hasten to laugh at everything, lest I should have to weep at everything"?

Ah! let Marie Antoinette pay attention and lend

her ear. At the moment when the trial of the necklace is beginning, and everywhere are circulating the malicious inventions of hate and falsehood, would one not say that almost all these calumnious lies are foretold by Basil: "Calumny! you don't know what it is you despise. I have seen the honestest people nearly crushed by it. Do you think that there is any stupid scandal, any horror, any absurd tale, which cannot be spread among the idlers of a great town with proper care? and we have to do here with crafty people." Beautiful and unfortunate Queen! So when she listened to this definition of the *crescendo* of calumny, must she not have grown pale? "First a faint rumor, skimming the ground like a swallow before the storm, murmurs *pianissimo*, and flits and drops the poisonous dart. A mouth picks it up, and *piano, piano*, drops it adroitly in some one's ear. The harm is done; it grows, spreads, makes its way *rinforzando*, from mouth to mouth, on its devilish path; then suddenly, no one knows how, you see calumny rise, hissing, and growing before your eyes. It spreads, takes flight, whirls about, covers everything, rends, tears, thunders, and becomes, with the aid of Heaven, a general cry, a public *crescendo*, a universal chorus of hate and denunciation. Who the devil could withstand it?"

With this performance of the "Barber of Seville," ended the theatricals at the Little Trianon. The day of comedies was over. What was preparing was a drama; not a stage drama, but a real one, a terrible one, in which Providence had prepared for the Queen the most tragic and touching part. The prologue was already beginning in this strange and fatal affair of the necklace, the plot of which recalls the most complicated plays. We shall try to set some of the characters on the stage

VI.

THE CARDINAL DE ROHAN.

THERE is no more curious trial than that about the necklace. It is a sort of romance, which seems the invention of calumny and hate; a strange mixture of seriousness and frivolity, as inexplicable as an enigma, as full of incident as a play; a tragi-comedy designed to pique and amuse the malevolence of the public; a plot more strange and improbable than even Beaumarchais could have invented; a prologue to the Revolution, one in which everything is a matter of surprise: the persons accused, the judges, the public, the investigation, the trial, the verdict.

Such a character as the Cardinal de Rohan can appear only in a society that is on the point of perishing. This priest, who is a man of the world, and cannot live on less than twelve hundred thousand francs a year; this bishop, prince, and ambassador, who changes his cassock for a hunting-coat, and prefers drawing-rooms and boudoirs to churches and sacristies; this ecclesiastical Don Juan, glittering in golden chasubles, whose pastoral ring is a jewel of inestimable value, whose lace rochets fill the most fashionable beauties with envy; this cardinal, who makes his appearance between a charlatan and a depraved woman, between a Cagliostro and a Madame de La Motte; this intelligent and foolish man, simple and corrupt, generous and most crafty, sceptical and incredulous, is surely a most characteristic figure. What dreams, what follies, haunt the imagination of this prince of the Church, who aspires to the glory of the great Richelieu and the good fortunes of the skilful Mazarin! What ambitions fire the brain of this dreamer who fancies himself on the point of discovering the philosopher's stone, and boasts that soon, thanks to the magical power of his friend Cagliostro, he is to become the mightiest and richest prince in the world! Beneath his aristocratic calm, under the reserve of good society, what excitement, what tempests, what delirium prevails! This man who makes his grand vicar write his charges, and writes his love-letters himself; who is more interested in a sorcerer's conjuring-book than in the holy words of the Church; this bishop, this cardinal, who, as if in scorn, is the Grand Almoner of France at the moment when the clergy, attacked by the philosophers, ought to be adding to its wisdom, its austerity, its virtue — this man is the incarnation of all the elegance and all the vices of the crumbling society.

Louis René Edouard de Rohan was born in 1734. His high rank raised him speedily to ecclesiastical dignity. When Marie Antoinette arrived in France, in 1770, to marry the Dauphin, he was the suffragan bishop of his uncle, the Cardinal Constantin de Rohan, Prince Bishop of Strasburg. In the absence of his uncle, who was ill, he received the Dauphiness at the cathedral door, and congratulated her.

The 21st of June, in the next year, Marie Antoinette wrote to her mother: "It is said that the suffragan bishop of Strasburg is to go to Vienna. He belongs to a very great family, but his life hitherto has been much more that of a soldier than of a bishop."

For her part, Maria Theresa wrote to the Count of Mercy, July 8: "I have every reason to be dissatisfied with the choice of such a worthless person for French Ambassador at this court. I should, perhaps, have refused to receive him, if I had not been withheld by the consideration of the annoyance to my daughter this action might call forth; but you must not neglect to let the French court know that it would do well to recommend to the Ambassador discreet behavior, such as becomes his position and the office he is to fill; and that, moreover, I should not be over-ready to wink at any extravagances or scandals in which he may be inclined to indulge."

Once in Vienna, Prince Louis, — for so the future cardinal was then styled, — displayed extraordinary pomp and luxury. His manner of life was regal: he kept a stable of fifty horses, had two state carriages which cost twenty thousand francs apiece, a first equerry, a sub-equerry, two grooms, seven pages of noble birth, with their tutor and guardian, two gentlemen to do the honors of the bedchamber, a head butler, a chief cook, two footmen, four running-footmen in gold livery, six valets de chambre, twelve footmen for the house, two porters, ten musicians clad in scarlet, a steward, a treasurer; finally, for the diplomatic work, four secretaries and four gentlemen. His gallantry was notorious. He was always at the theatre. He used to wear the different hunting-uniforms of the noblemen whom he visited.

One Corpus Christi Day, he and all the Embassy, in their green uniforms slashed with gold, broke through a procession which blocked their path, in order to join a hunting-party given by the Prince of Paar. His prodigality was excessive, and the conduct of his suite was most scandalous. Maria Theresa hated him as if she had a presentiment of the harm he was to do Marie Antoinette. The Empress wrote to the Count of Mercy-Argenteau, January 19, 1772: "I cannot express approval of the Ambassador Rohan. He is a huge volume of evil language which is ill suited to his position as ecclesiastic and as minister; he lets it flow in the most impudent way on every occasion, with no knowledge of affairs and without the necessary gifts, but full of levity, presumption, and indifference. . . . His suite is also a collection of people destitute of merit and of morals."

Every day Maria Theresa complained more bitterly. She wrote again to the Count of Mercy, March 18, 1772: " The Prince de Rohan displeases me more and more; he is a worthless fellow. . . .

To be sure, the Emperor likes to talk with him, but it is only to draw out his stupid, bragging chatter." September 1 of the same year: "Rohan is always the same; yet nearly all our women, young and old, pretty or plain, are none the less fascinated by this extravagant and ridiculous villain." May 15, 1773: "The sooner Rohan is recalled, the better pleased I shall be. He is unendurable." And in July: "There is no need of hoping for any change in the conduct of the Prince de Rohan. He is incorrigible, and his servants, the rascals, are just like their worthless master. They corrupt my people, exactly as their master corrupts the nobility. Their insolence goes to the wildest excesses and fills my subjects with indignation."

It was during his embassy in Vienna that Rohan lost the friendship of Marie Antoinette. One evening, Madame Du Barry read aloud, at the King's supper-table, in the Dauphin's presence, a letter in which the Ambassador described the Empress Maria Theresa as holding in one hand a handkerchief with which to wipe away the tears she was shedding over the woes of Poland, while in the other she was holding a sword wherewith to divide that unfortunate country. The letter, which was a confidential one, had been written, not to Madame Du Barry, but to the Duke of Aiguillon. Marie Antoinette, however, thought that it was written to the Countess, and could not forgive the Ambassador for choosing such a correspondent or for presuming to criticise Maria Theresa.

The Prince de Rohan held the post of ambassador for only two years. When Louis XVI. ascended the throne, Rohan appeared to be in disgrace, which, however, did not prevent his being loaded with honors. A relative of his, the Countess of Marsan, who had brought up the King, succeeded by her insistence in having him appointed Grand Almoner of France, on the death of the Cardinal de La Roche-Aymon, in 1777. Then he became Prince Bishop of Strasburg, in 1779, on the death of his uncle, whose suffragan he had been. He obtained his cardinal's hat through the favor of Stanislas Poniatowski, King of Poland, and the abbey of Saint Waast, with its enormous revenues. He was admitted to the French Academy, and chosen Principal of the Sorbonne. This last position, which was much sought after by the high dignitaries of the Church, was filled by the votes of the graduate ecclesiastics and the doctors of the Sorbonne. The cardinals did their best to secure this post at the head of this famous institution, the sanctuary of theology, the stronghold of religion; but the Grand Almoner succeeded over all his rivals.

Part of the time he lived in Paris, in a splendid mansion in the rue Vieille du Temple, which is now the National Printing-house, and part of the time at Saverne, in a magnificent palace. The Baroness Oberkirch, who visited him there in 1780, was much struck by the pomp he displayed. She describes him as handsome, polite, majestic, coming out of his chapel in a cassock of scarlet watered silk and an English rochet of inestimable value. When he officiated at Versailles he wore an alb, for great ceremonies, of such valuable lace that one hardly dared touch it; his arms and motto were arranged in medallions above large flowers, and it was estimated to be worth a hundred thousand francs. In his hand he carried an illuminated missal, a family heirloom, of royal magnificence. "He came to meet us," Madame d'Oberkirch goes on, "with an air of a great lord's gallantry and politeness such as I have seldom seen. The Cardinal was highly educated and very amiable."

This handsome prelate, so rich and flattered, fancied himself a victim of fate. As Grand Almoner of France, he was at the head of the episcopate and the clergy; no bishop could see the King except with his permission; he held the patronage of all the positions as King's almoners, eight in number, and those as chaplains, with their large livings. He was not satisfied with being a Prince of the House of Rohan, Cardinal, Grand Almoner of France, a Knight of the Holy Ghost, Bishop of Strasburg, Sovereign Prince of Hildesheim, Abbot of Noirmoutiers and of Saint Waast, Principal of the Sorbonne, Superior of the Asylum for the Blind, the possessor of an income of from seven to eight hundred thousand francs from the revenues of the Church, a member of the French Academy, a man of the highest fashion, the favorite of all the fine ladies of the courts of Vienna and Versailles: this ambitious man wanted something more. What he asked of fate, what he was surprised that he did not yet possess, was the unlimited power and rank of prime minister, the joy of seeing all his rivals at his feet.

What prevented the realization of this vision of pride and glory? Only one person, he thought, — the Queen. How could he, so glorious and fascinating, he, the Cardinal Prince of Rohan, not succeed in making the conquest of a woman? In that, he said to himself in his fatuity, there was something really inexplicable. He, the Prince of Rohan, not please the Queen! There must be some mistake. Yet Marie Antoinette continued to maintain her icy attitude. She never addressed a word to the Grand Almoner of France. The Grand Almoner lamented it. He would gladly have given all his revenues from the Church for a word, for a smile. This disdain of Marie Antoinette's was the torture, the despair of the Cardinal. His most ardent desire was to become her favorite; that was the aim to which all the resources of his mind were turned. When he was seeking with a feverish anxiety every means to obtain the good graces of his sovereign and to reach the summit of fortune, of greatness, he met two persons who, he thought, could be of the greatest service to him in carrying out his design — a charlatan and an intriguing woman, Cagliostro and Madame de La Motte.

VII.

CAGLIOSTRO.

WHEN we cease to study history superficially and go down into its depths, we are surprised at the supply of absurdities which every period adds to the mass of human follies, and we acquire the conviction that what we call common sense ought to be called the uncommon sense. The illogicality, the contradictions, the absurdities, of the human heart are eternal causes of surprise. The more corrupt the society, the more easily is it led to every extravagance in its tastes and fashions.

Superstition and incredulity walk hand in hand; men refuse to believe in the Gospel, only to give their faith to the wildest chimeras, the most eccentric visions; they call themselves hard-headed, and suffer from every weakness; they boast that they are followers of reason, and they are in fact only apostles of madness; they cease to believe in God, but they still believe in the devil. Extremes meet, and old races have all the credulity of children. The mania for the supernatural, the rage for the marvellous, prevailed in the last years of the eighteenth century, which had wantonly derided every sacred thing. Never were the Rosicrucians, the adepts, sorcerers, and prophets so numerous and so respected. Serious and educated men, magistrates, courtiers, declared themselves eye-witnesses of alleged miracles. "I have a theory," said the Prince of Ligne, "that the most reasonable persons have, unknown to themselves, a romantic corner in their life. No one of us escapes it; it is the tribute we pay to the imagination."

When Cagliostro came to France, he found the ground prepared for his magical operations. A society eager for distractions and emotions, indulgent to every form of extravagance, necessarily welcomed such a man and hailed him as its guide. Whence did he come? What was his country, his age, his origin? Where did he get those extraordinary diamonds which adorned his dress, the gold which he squandered so freely? It was all a mystery. Like his predecessor, the Count of Saint Germain, he pretended to be more than three hundred years old, while he seemed to be about thirty. It was, he said, because he possessed the secret of eternal youth and the power of reawakening love. With him was his young wife, a beautiful Neapolitan, the Flower of Vesuvius, as she was called, Serafina Feliciani.

So far as was known, Cagliostro had no resources, no letter of credit, and yet he lived in luxury. He treated and cured the poor without pay, and not satisfied with restoring them to health, he made them large presents of money. His generosity to the poor, his scorn for the great, aroused universal enthusiasm. The Germans, who lived on legends, imagined that he was the Wandering Jew. When he first set foot on French soil, in 1780, he chose Strasburg for his residence, being attracted thither by the Cathedral spire. The Cardinal de Rohan, who was then living in his splendid castle at Saverne, in more than princely luxury, was extremely anxious to become acquainted with the famous worker of wonders. Cagliostro did not make the first steps: "If the Cardinal is sick," he said, "he may come to me, and I will cure him; if he is well, he has no need for me, nor I for him." This charlatan, who gave out that he had discovered the philosopher's stone, understood how to extract inexhaustible supplies from the devotion of his adherents. He asked for nothing, and received everything in abundance. They gave everything to him, under the impression that they were enriching themselves. The Egyptian lodges which he founded everywhere he went, brought him in large revenues. He exercised a real fascination on his adepts.

The Baroness of Oberkirch, who saw him at Saverne in 1780, at the Cardinal's palace, has described the adoration which was paid him: "No one can ever form the faintest idea of the fervor with which everybody pursued Cagliostro. He was surrounded, besieged; every one trying to win a glance or a word. ... A dozen ladies of rank and two actresses had followed him, in order to continue their treatment.

. . . If I had not seen it, I should never have imagined that a prince of the Roman Church, a Rohan, a man in other respects intelligent and honorable, could so far let himself be imposed upon as to renounce his dignity, his free will, at the bidding of a sharper."

One day Cagliostro said to the Cardinal, "Your soul is worthy of mine, and you deserve to be the confidant of all my secrets." For his part, the Cardinal was never weary of expatiating on the merits of his new friend. He showed to the Baroness of Oberkirch a large stone which he wore on his little finger, on which was cut the coat-of-arms of the house of Rohan; it was worth twenty thousand francs at the lowest calculation. "It's a beautiful stone, Your Grace," said the Baroness; "I have often admired it." "Well, he made it," the Cardinal went on; "he made it, and out of nothing; I saw him with my own eyes; I was there watching the crucible; I was present at the operation. Is that science? What do you think? You mustn't say that he is deceiving me, for the jeweller and the engraver set the value of the stone at twenty-five thousand francs. You must acknowledge that it is a singular swindler who makes presents like that." Then, growing more excited, the Cardinal added with great warmth: "That's not all; he makes gold; he has made five or six thousand francs' worth before me, up there in the top of the palace. I am to have more; I am to have a great deal; he will make me the richest prince in Europe.

These are not dreams, Madame; they are proofs. And his prophecies that have come true! and the miraculous cures he has wrought! I tell you he is the most extraordinary, the sublimest man in the world, and his knowledge is equalled only by his kindness. How much he gives in alms! How much good he does! It passes all imagination!"

Cagliostro did not content himself with promising the Cardinal glory and power; he also cured him of an asthma: consequently nothing equalled the gratitude of this prince of the Church. He spoke with affection and admiration of this wonderful man, whom he regarded as his guide and saviour. From that moment Cagliostro was free to help himself from the purse of this showy and generous prelate. January 30, 1785, he took up his quarters in Paris, at the Marais, in the rue Saint Claude, very near the Cardinal's residence. Paris was no less enthusiastic than Strasburg. With his half-philosophical, half-mystical jargon, his knowledge of physics, chemistry, alchemy, and medicine; his pretence of making gold, of having lived in past centuries, of foretelling the future, and of having guessed the great secrets of creation, Cagliostro upset and fired feeble minds. His glance, at one moment all flame, the next ice, fascinated them. To the sick he used to say, "I will give you health"; to the poor, "I will give you wealth"; to the impotent, "I will give you love."

Flattering the sensuality of the age, he exalted the natural instincts as beneficent emanations granted to mortals by the Supreme Being, as a recompense for the evils inseparable from humanity. He taught that the religion most worthy of God and of man was that of the patriarchs, and that Adam, Seth, Enoch, Noah, Abraham, Isaac, Jacob, had lived in close intimacy with their Creator, who continually manifested himself to them. He added that he was the possessor of this secret of the patriarchs, and that, like them, he was in direct and continual communication with Him. Speaking a strange gibberish, which was neither French nor Italian, with which he mingled a jargon which he did not translate, but called Arabic, he used to recite with solemn emphasis the most absurd fables. When he repeated his conversation with the angel of light and the angel of darkness, when he spoke of the great secret of Memphis, of the Hierophant, of the giants, the enormous animals, of a city in the interior of Africa ten times as large as Paris, where his correspondents lived, he found a number of people ready to listen and to believe him.

In his medical treatment, his three great panaceas were baths in which there was a great quantity of the extract of Saturn; a potion, of which the receipt was in the hands only of an apothecary he had chosen; and some drops of his own composition, the miraculous effects of which, he said, would cure all the diseases which physicians had pronounced hopeless.

As a sorcerer he had a cabalistic apparatus. On a table with a black cloth, on which were embroidered in red the mysterious signs of the highest degree of the Rosicrucians, there stood the emblems: little Egyptian figures, old vials filled with lustral waters, and a crucifix, very like, though not the same as the Christian's cross; and there too Cagliostro placed a glass globe full of clarified water. Before the globe he used to place a kneeling seer; that is to say, a young woman who, by supernatural powers, should behold the scenes which were believed to take place in water within the magic globe.

Count Beugnot, who gives all the details in his Memoirs, adds that for the proper performance of the miracle, the seer had to be of angelic purity, to have been born under a certain constellation, to have delicate nerves, great sensitiveness, and, in addition, blue eyes. When she had knelt down, the geniuses were bidden to enter the globe. The water became active and turbid. The seer was convulsed, she ground her teeth, and exhibited every sign of nervous excitement. At last she saw and began to speak. What was taking place that very moment at hundreds of miles from Paris, in Vienna or Saint Petersburg, in America or Pekin, as well as things which were going to occur only some weeks, months, or years later, she declared that she saw distinctly in the globe. The operation had succeeded; the adepts were transported with delight.

"It would be hard," says Count Beugnot, "to believe that such scenes could have place in France at the end of the eighteenth century; yet they aroused great interest among people of importance in the court and the town. The Count of Estaing allowed himself to be led away by these follies, and became their upholder. The Cardinal de Rohan was amazed at the power these prophecies gave him over his enemies, and he let it be known that the Duke of Chartres, whose court had decided not to believe in God, was ready to believe in Cagliostro; so true it is, that in human weakness there is always an opening for faith, which is always likely, when it lacks proper material. to tolerate ridiculous or dangerous subjects."

Cagliostro was certainly one of the main causes of the misfortunes of the Cardinal de Rohan. Such an oracle was sure to ruin the ambitious prelate, by driving him to delirium through fantastic promises of power, wealth, and love. When the fatal business of the purchase of the necklace came up, Cagliostro, who had recently come to Paris, was mysteriously consulted in the very drawing-room of the Cardinal. The Egyptian invocations took place in the light of countless candles. The prophet ascended the tripod and spoke. The matter, he declared, was worthy of the Prince; it would be completely successful; it would put the last touch to the kindness of the Queen, and finally hasten the day when, for the happiness of France, of Europe, of humanity, the rare gifts of the Cardinal should become known. Rohan hesitated no longer, and the affair of the necklace began.

VIII.

THE COUNTESS DE LA MOTTE.

THE Countess de La Motte was, even more than Cagliostro, the evil genius of the Cardinal de Rohan. She was a perfect type of a woman of no defined position, at war, from her birth, with the social order, all the laws of which she defied; she was an adventuress, who united with vicious instincts wild extravagance, and insatiable vanity with the haughtiness of a princess, the cynicism and depravity of a courtesan. Madame de La Motte was one of those unhappy natures which show what intelligence is when not controlled by morality and common sense. This woman, whose ardent imagination had a demoniac quality, found that at certain limits lying is a proof of ability; imposture, of courage; swindling, of talent. She appeared on the scene as if by a mockery of fate, and she it was who, for the last time, evoked before the multitude a name famous throughout the world. The blood of Henri II., the lover of Diane de Poitiers, flowed in her veins. Strange are the vicissitudes of destiny! This race of the Valois, once so powerful, was represented by this woman. What a delight for the secret enemies of the throne! What scandals they concocted! The Valois slandering the Bourbons; the two families engaged in the same trial; the adulteries of Henri II. punished in his illegitimate progeny; what an irony of fate! what a prologue of the Revolution!

Jeanne de Saint-Remy de Valois, Countess de La Motte, was born at Fontette (Aube), July 22, 1756. She was the second child of Jacques de Saint-Remy de Valois, and descended in the seventh generation from Henri de Saint-Remy, son of Henri II., King of France, and of Nicole de Savigny, Lady de Saint-Remy, de Fontette, du Châtelier, and de Noëz. In spite of its illustrious origin, this family had long been extremely poor. One of its members made answer to Louis XIII., who asked him what he was doing at his estate, "Sire, I am only doing what I should do." Later the true meaning of this seemingly haughty reply came out, when it was discovered that this descendant of the Valois was making, on his estate, counterfeit money wherewith to pay his numerous creditors.

The father of Madame de La Motte was sunk in the deepest misery. He had married the daughter of the concierge of his Fontette house, by whom he had four children, one son and three daughters. He died in a hospital in 1762. A charitable lady, the Marchioness of Boulainvilliers, took charge of the children, sent the boy to a naval school, and the girls to a boarding-school at Passy. Their genealogy was verified by d'Hozier in 1776, and the King allowed to each one of the children a pension of eight hundred francs. But a young, ambitious girl, fond of luxury and dress, could not live on any such sum as that. Jeanne desired to make her fortune, and any way was good for her. She spent a year at Bar-sur-Aube, with a lady named Surmont, and then married a gentleman as poor as herself, the Count de La Motte, a gendarme (at that time the gendarmes were the first regiment of cavalry; the privates who belonged to it had the rank of officers and could obtain the cross of Saint Louis).

In 1782, the pair came to Paris, took up their abode in furnished lodgings in the rue de la Verrerie, where they lived in great poverty; in 1783, they were compelled to deposit their furniture with a wig-maker, through fear of the bailiff. Early in 1784, Madame de La Motte pledged her dresses and belongings at the pawnbroker's. She was reduced to extreme poverty when suddenly a change came. All at once this woman who lived on charity had abundance of money. This is what had happened. Madame de La Motte had had an audience with the Cardinal de Rohan, and had besought him to transmit a petition to the King. The Cardinal thought his suppliant very pretty, and became interested in her fate. He was still more surprised when he learned in what want the court left the descendants of Henri II. The petitioner's strongest arguments were her trim figure, her expressive blue eyes beneath arching black eyebrows, her fine teeth, her little foot, her aristocratic hand, her marvellously fair complexion.

The prelate was fascinated; the bold adventuress saw that she had at last found her prey. Living in the days of society where smooth rascals regarded the most detestable villanies as excellent plans, she had chosen for her secretary, or rather for her accomplice, an old fellow-soldier of her husband in the gendarmerie, a certain Rétaux de Villette, who then was prowling between Paris and Versailles with no definite means of subsistence. This supple and insinuating man, who at any rate knew enough to turn off a letter, was required by Madame de La Motte for the correspondences she was soon to undertake.

Her plan was soon made. The Cardinal was a libertine, she would address his passions; he was thoroughly ambitious, she would direct that feeling. The prelate had confided to her that his grief, his torture, what poisoned all his happiness, was being in disgrace with Marie Antoinette. What would he not be willing to pay any one who would bring about a reconciliation with the Queen? He said to himself that if he should become the favorite of Marie Antoinette, he would thereby be the absolute master of France, the Mazarin of a new Anne of Austria. This thought drove him almost wild, as Madame de La Motte saw, and she at once devised the means of ruining him. She suddenly pretended that her lot had changed, that fortune was smiling on her, that she had had many audiences with the Queen, and that Her Majesty had conferred many benefits on her, had made her a confidante, and wrote to her letters full of the most amiable feeling.

This bold adventuress showed these pretended letters, which were written by a forger, to every comer, and offered her protection to her credulous victims. She convinced the Cardinal that she often spoke of him to the Queen, that she pleaded his cause with great skill, and that gradually she was bringing him to a high place in Her Majesty's favor. "The Queen," she said to him, "has commissioned me to ask you to give me your justification in writing." The prelate, full of hope at once, composed with eagerness the required apology, and Madame de La Motte told him that this memorial, which she had herself presented to Marie Antoinette, had done wonders. The Queen, she went on, asked of her future favorite only a little patience and a little discretion; but the day was drawing nigh when she should be able to throw aside the mask and to make a public announcement of the high positions to which he was to be called. Madame de La Motte urged the prelate to notice the Queen on such or such a day, at such or such an hour, when she should be entering the hall of the Œil de Bœuf; Her Majesty would make him a sign with her head, which would confirm his hopes.

The Grand Almoner, full of delight, noticed in fact that the Queen had moved her head, which was not at all surprising; and he was fatuous enough to imagine that this movement was the appointed signal mentioned by Madame de La Motte. What this adventuress now needed for the further carrying out of her devilish plot was a few sheets of gilt-edged letter paper. With these, aided by her customary accomplice, she forged a series of letters from the Queen to the Cardinal, who received with joy these alleged royal letters, and wrote answers which he thought that Madame de La Motte gave to the Queen. All this was in the months of May, June, and July, 1784. Madame de La Motte had a banker in the Cardinal, but all his revenues and treasures were scarcely sufficient to pay the debt of his gratitude. Was there anything too fine for a Valois, for a woman who reconciled a man of his genius with his sovereign. It would be a mistake to suppose that Madame de La Motte's luxury began only after the theft of the necklace. Nine months earlier, she was living extravagantly, thanks to two gifts of sixty thousand francs each, from the fund of the Grand Almoner and to a sum of thirty thousand francs assigned to her from the Cardinal's private purse.

The fraud was everywhere triumphant, and yet Madame de La Motte was uneasy. Blind as he was, might not the Cardinal sooner or later discover the truth? Would he not notice the irregular and almost inexplicable contrast between the more than affectionate tone of the alleged letters of the Queen, and the cold, reserved, almost icy attitude which she maintained in public before the man who already imagined himself her favorite? In the correspondence which passed through the hands of Madame de La Motte, the Cardinal was continually begging for an audience, which was always promised but never granted; and in spite of his blindness might he not form some vague suspicion? This danger had to be met; it was necessary to find something that should absolutely corroborate his mistaken views, and make him sure that he had heard with his own ears, seen with his own eyes. Hence the scene in the grove, one of the most curious incidents of this strange and eventful drama.

It was July, 1784. The first performance of the "Marriage of Figaro" had taken place on the 27th of the previous April. The final scene, the nocturnal confusion under the shadows of the avenue of the chestnut-trees, had made a great impression, and it was possibly the sight of this that suggested to Madame de La Motte the first idea of the scene in the grove at Versailles. Her husband, strolling in the garden of the Palais Royal, had met a woman who in face and figure somewhat resembled the Queen. The likeness struck him, and he mentioned it to his wife, who bade him make the woman's acquaintance. She was a Miss d'Oliva, a woman of doubtful repute, who occupied a small apartment in the rue du Jour, near Saint Eustache. M. de La Motte followed her, made her several visits, and one evening told her that a woman of quality, a countess, who had often heard of her, would be brought to see her the next day.

This was done, and Madame de La Motte had no difficulty in cajoling the poor girl. She showed her the pretended letters of the Queen; "You see," she said, "I am in Her Majesty's confidence. She has just given me a new proof of it, by asking me to find some one who can do something for her which will be explained at the proper time. I come to propose it to you. If you consent, I will make you a present of fifteen thousand francs, and the Queen will make you an even larger present. I can't tell you now who I am, but you shall soon know." The d'Oliva was naturally delighted with such a windfall, and accepted without hesitation. The next day M. de La Motte went to her rooms for her, in the afternoon, and carried her with him to Versailles, to the Hôtel de la Belle Image, Place Dauphin. The next day Madame de La Motte instructed her ignorant accomplice in the part she was to play. She began by making her put on a white dress trimmed with red, and to throw over her head a thing called a *thérèse*. Then she gave her the necessary directions: "This evening I shall take you to the park; a great nobleman will come up to you, and you will give him this letter, and this rose, saying nothing but this, 'You know what this means'; that is all you will have to do." The d'Oliva, who was convinced that this little scene was desired by the Queen, for her own amusement, had no other thought than to play her part to the best of her ability.

This was July 28, 1784. The Cardinal had received word from Madame de La Motte, to be that evening, at about ten o'clock, in the Versailles park, near the grove of Venus, where the Queen would at last grant him the interview he had so long desired.

It was a very dark night; no sound disturbed the mysterious silence of the park; the Cardinal, full of hope, his imagination aglow with Heaven knows what visions of pride and pleasure, was eagerly awaiting the pretended rendezvous, the hour of triumph, the blissful moment, when the royal apparition should appear beneath the dark trees. Never had more romantic dreams fired a man's ardent brain. Suddenly the Cardinal's more than amorous impatience was interrupted by the rustle of a dress. It was, he thought, the Queen of France and of Navarre, the majestic, poetic, enchanting Marie Antoinette, the first woman of the world. As soon as he saw the d'Oliva, whom he took for the Queen, he bowed low, murmuring some few words. The d'Oliva replied by offering him a rose, and saying in a voice broken by emotion, "You know what this means." Then Madame de La Motte appeared. "Come quick, quick!" she exclaimed. Rétaux de Villette said, as if in alarm, "Here is the Countess of Artois!" The d'Oliva disappeared like a shadow, and all was silent again.

The Cardinal thought himself the happiest man in the world. Not only, he imagined, had the Queen pardoned him, but, as if by miracle, she had passed from hate to sympathy, and from sympathy to love. In proof of this tender feeling, she had given him a rose: a mystic gift! a cherished token! This rose he covered with ardent kisses; he placed it with devotion on his heart. He fancied himself transported to a delightful spot, some happy Eden, to a world of ineffable bliss. What he felt was no longer joy, intoxication, delirium; it was ecstasy. The mystification had succeeded even beyond Madame de La Motte's hopes.

The next day the d'Oliva was shown an alleged letter from the Queen, which ran thus: "My dear Countess, I am delighted with the woman you selected; she played her part to perfection, and her future is assured."

Some time later Madame de La Motte gave the Cardinal forged letters of the Queen, and asked him for one hundred and fifty thousand francs in behalf of persons in whom she was interested. He hastened to give her the amount. The bold adventuress betook herself to Bar-sur-Aube with all this money, to dazzle the eyes of her old friends. Her house was filled with silverware, fine furniture, china, and jewels. She drove with four horses. In playing the princess, she was always accompanied by four lackeys carrying lighted torches, and by a negro all covered with silver. There could be no better preparation for some immense fraud, and Madame de La Motte thought that the time was ripe for carrying through the swindle of the necklace.

IX.

THE NECKLACE.

THE famous affair of the necklace, which has been the subject of many commentaries and many hot discussions, is no longer obscure. A very careful student, M. Emile Compardon, has made it perfectly clear in a work which is corroborated in everything it says by the proceedings which took place before the Parliament of Paris.

"To show that the diamond necklace, purchased in the name of Marie Antoinette, but without her knowledge, by the Cardinal de Rohan, was stolen, taken apart, and sold by the Count and Countess de La Motte-Valois;

"To prove this by the critical examination of the proceedings before the Parliament of Paris in this unhappy matter;

"To purge the Queen of the calumnies of her contemporaries, which have been echoed by some later historians,"—such is the aim which M. Compardon set himself in writing his book, *Marie Antoinette and the Case of the Necklace*. He has fully succeeded in his intention; and the more closely the affair is studied, the juster and more fitting are the historian's conclusions.

The Abbé Georgel, Grand Vicar of the Cardinal de Rohan, and the author of the curious Memoirs already mentioned, mentions at the end of his account the four points below, as proved at the trial:—

1. The Cardinal had been convinced that he was buying the necklace for the Queen.

2. The authorization, signed "Marie Antoinette, of France," was really written by Villette, who committed this forgery at the instigation of Madame de La Motte.

3. The necklace was delivered to this lady.

4. Her husband carried it, taken apart, to London, and sold the most valuable of the jewels for his own profit.

Thanks to the Memoirs of the Abbé Georgel, of Madame Campan, of the Count Beugnot; thanks to the examination of the Cardinal de Rohan, of Madame de La Motte, of Cagliostro, of the d'Oliva, of Rétaux de Villette, and to M. Compardon's clear and thorough book, all doubts are scattered and the truth is brought to light.

Let us begin with saying where it was that the necklace, which was destined to make so great a scandal, came from. The crown-jewellers, Boehmer and Bassenge, had made it by stringing together the most valuable diamonds on sale. Unfortunately for these men, diamonds had rather gone out of fashion in the French court. In that period of eclogues and idyls which was the prelude to such horrible tragedies, simplicity was all the rage. Marie Antoinette used to wear a dress of white linen, and a shepherdess's, preferring natural flowers to the most magnificent jewels. Nevertheless, the jewellers persuaded the first gentleman-in-waiting to show the necklace to Louis XVI., who was delighted with it, and had it shown to Marie Antoinette.

The Queen thought the necklace very handsome, as, in fact, it was; but she was averse to having any such sum spent upon her. Michelet says: "Royalty, as a religion, as a permanent miracle, requires glittering, dazzling splendors. The strange sparkles of a diamond serve as a fairy-like mystery, an aureole." Such was not Marie Antoinette's opinion. She said that diamonds were worn at court only about three or four times a year, that she already had enough, and that the money which the necklace would cost had better be spent in building a vessel of the state, which would be much more useful. Boehmer, one of the jewellers, was in despair at this refusal. He obtained an audience with the Queen, and told her, in great distress, that he should be ruined, and would drown himself, if the necklace were not bought. The Queen said to him: "The King wanted to give me the necklace; I declined it; so don't speak to me about it. Try to take it apart, and to sell it piecemeal; and don't drown yourself."

This was in December, 1778. The Queen had just given birth to her first child, Madame Royale (later the Duchess of Angoulême), and Boehmer had hoped that the Queen would be glad to receive the necklace as a present on her recovery. The unhappy man's deception was cruel. He had staked all his fortune on this unrivalled ornament, and the idea of taking it apart shocked equally his tastes as an artist and his interests as a tradesman. He visited all the principal cities of Europe, in the hope of finding a purchaser for this marvel, but everywhere its high price — one million six hundred thousand francs — prevented his selling it.

In the spring of 1785 preparations were made at Versailles to celebrate the baptism of the Duke of Angoulême, the son of the Count of Artois. On this occasion Louis XVI. and Marie Antoinette presented the little prince with a shoulder-knot, buckles, and a sword set with diamonds. Boehmer, as crown-jeweller, was to supply the different objects. When he delivered them to the Queen, he handed her a letter which ran thus: "Madame, we are perfectly happy at being allowed to think that the last arrangements which have been proposed to us, and to which we have consented with all zeal and respect, are a new proof of our submission and our devotion to Your Majesty's orders, and we take the profoundest satisfaction in thinking that the most sumptuous array of diamonds in the world will belong to the best and most beautiful of queens."

Marie Antoinette, who could not understand this letter in the least, sent some one to recall the jeweller, that he might explain it; but he had disappeared. The Queen then said that the letter was another proof of Boehmer's addled wits, and, wanting to seal some letters, she burned it at the flame of a candle at her side. "There is no need to keep it," she said to Madame Campan; then she went on: "This man always has a bee in his bonnet. Be sure and tell him, the first time you see him, that I don't care for diamonds any more, and that I shall never buy any more; that, if I had to spend any money, I should much prefer enlarging the place at Saint Cloud by buying some of the land adjoining it. Go into all these details with him to convince him and impress it upon him." Madame Campan asked, "Does Your Majesty wish me to have him come to see me?" "No," answered the Queen; "it will do very well the first time you see him."

A few days later, August 3, 1785, Madame Campan was at Crespy, at her father-in-law's, who gave a dinner-party every Sunday. Boehmer used to come once or twice every Sunday, and he happened to come on that day. Madame Campan took advantage of the opportunity to give him the Queen's message. The jeweller was amazed. "There is some mystery here," he cried; "I beg that you will let me have a talk with you, to explain the matter to you." They had their talk that evening, in the garden, when the other guests had left for Paris. The strange revelation filled Madame Campan with horror. She saw the horrible snare set for the Queen's reputation, and she was so surprised and so affected that it began to rain and to thunder without her noticing it.

Boehmer was not mad: like the Cardinal de Rohan, he had been the dupe of the boldest and most infamous intrigue.

What had happened? At the end of the previous year, Madame de La Motte, who was always on the lookout for new frauds, had seen that the necklace might be the occasion of an unprecedented swindle, and her fertile imagination had been turned towards carrying it out.

January 21, 1785, she had told Boehmer's partner that the Queen desired to purchase the necklace, which she had long wanted; but that, being averse to treating directly with the jewellers, she had entrusted the matter to a certain great nobleman. Madame de La Motte added that she advised them to take every precaution with regard to this eminent personage.

This eminent personage was the Cardinal de Rohan. What had the bold adventuress done? By means of a steady fire of forged letters, she had succeeded in persuading the prelate that the Queen ardently desired the necklace, and that since she wished to get possession of it without her husband's knowledge and pay for it in instalments out of the money she might save from her own expenses, she gave the Grand Almoner a special proof of friendliness by entrusting the purchase to him. He was to receive, Madame de La Motte added, an authorization written and signed by the Queen, and he would have to arrange with the jewellers for the terms of payment. In the transaction, which was to be concluded by the Cardinal alone, the Queen was not to be mentioned. Was not the secret authorization, signed by the Queen, a sufficient guarantee, Madame de La Motte asked, and did not the Queen thereby give the Cardinal a token of exceptional confidence?

The prelate, still under the impression of the scene in the garden, did not hesitate for a moment. Besides, Cagliostro had declared that the matter was quite worthy of the Cardinal, and that it would be the prelude to a whole series of triumphs in different directions.

January 29, Boehmer and Bassenge went to the Cardinal's palace, rue Vieille du Temple, and signed a paper containing the conditions of the sale. The price of the necklace was one million six hundred thousand francs, payable in four instalments, at intervals of four months.

January 31, Boehmer and Bassenge returned to the Cardinal's palace. The prelate showed them the contract, bearing the word "Approved," and the signature "Marie Antoinette de France," both the handiwork of Madame de La Motte's usual forger. The affair was concluded, and the jewellers departed blissfully happy.

The next day, February 1, the Cardinal, to whom the necklace had been delivered, went to Versailles, to the little lodging which Madame de La Motte occupied in the Place Dauphin; he was accompanied by a servant, who carried the necklace in its case. The Cardinal had just handed it to Madame de La Motte, when she told him that the alleged confidential agent of the Queen was coming; the Cardinal concealed himself in a closet with a glass door, and saw Madame de La Motte hand the case to Marie Antoinette's alleged messenger. The fraud was accomplished.

From that day forth the de La Mottes lived in luxury, satisfying every desire, every whim. The golden stream was never dry. The source of their wealth was the necklace. This marvellous work of art, which the jewellers were surprised to observe that the Queen never wore, had been taken apart. Madame de La Motte kept for herself the small gems, those that could not be recognized, and the large ones she had sold in London. Monsieur Compardon has proved these sales from the original documents; the statements of the English jewellers who bought them remove every doubt. Besides, can it be maintained for a moment that if the Queen had had this necklace in her possession, she would not have worn it?

Madame de La Motte was enraptured with the success of her fraud, and plunged into ever wilder extravagance; but the hour of justice was approaching. Boehmer had learned all the truth from Madame Campan. He went straightway to Breteuil, the Minister, and revealed part of the story, mentioning the Cardinal. but saying nothing about Madame de La

Motte. August 17, when the Queen was rehearsing the part of Rosina for the early performance of the "Barber of Seville," in the theatre of the Little Trianon, Madame Campan told her all she had learned from her talk with Boehmer. Marie Antoinette was filled with righteous indignation. "These hideous vices," she exclaimed, "must be unmasked. When the Roman purple and the title of prince conceal only a needy man, a swindler, who dares to compromise his sovereign's wife, all France and Europe must know it." August 9, Boehmer gave the Queen a written statement of the affair. August 15, at Versailles, in the Gallery of Mirrors, at the moment when the Cardinal, in his pontifical robes, was about to go to the chapel, he was arrested.

X.

THE ARREST.

AT first the affair of the necklace seemed to be a wholly inexplicable enigma. The imagination of a dramatist or of a novelist accustomed to the wildest inventions could have conceived nothing stranger. The first suggestion was that the Cardinal de Rohan, who, in spite of his colossal fortune and enormous revenues, owed many millions, had appropriated the necklace to fill his purse, and to make good the deficit in the administration of the Blind Asylum. As to the idea that a prince of the house of Rohan, a former ambassador, a cardinal, a grand almoner of France, a principal of the Sorbonne, a member of the French Academy, an educated and intelligent man, could for more than a year have imagined himself the confidential agent, the favorite, of a queen who never spoke a word to him, it never crossed any one's mind. It was inconceivable that a man of such importance could have been the victim of such a stupid, such a clumsy fraud.

More than one historian has blamed Marie Antoinette for not having suppressed the affair. But was that an easy thing to do? The Cardinal was still convinced that he had not been deceived, that the Queen's letters were genuine; that he had seen the Queen with his own eyes that evening in the garden, otherwise would he have consented to pay the one million six hundred thousand francs, demanded by Boehmer? What part, in that case, would Marie Antoinette have played in the eyes of her jewellers and their numerous confidants? To hush up the matter would have been equivalent to a confession of guilt and a corroboration of the supposition that there existed a shameful intrigue between the Queen of France and a licentious prelate. Marie Antoinette's proud and loyal nature rejected such a course with dignity. And could a sense of religious decorum allow the entrusting of such a cardinal with the functions of Grand Almoner? Could he continue to officiate at great ceremonies in this Versailles chapel, where his presence would be an insult to altar and throne? Should such a priest baptize the royal children! give the holy communion to the Very Christian King and Queen, and have charge of the religious instruction of the royal family and the court? And how could he be disgraced without making his fault public, without throwing a full light on the blackness of such a plot?

The Baron de Breteuil and the Abbé de Vermond, who were enemies of the Cardinal, had no difficulty in convincing the Queen that it was her duty once for all to put an end to this combination of secret calumny and hidden intrigue, an invisible but deadly network, in which wretches were endeavoring to envelop her reputation. The blood of Maria Theresa flowed in the veins of this daughter of the Cæsars. She had a feeling of indignation and wrath which carried away the most good-natured of kings. Made more beautiful by her tears and her emotion, Marie Antoinette, calumniated and insulted, as Queen and as a woman, asked justice from her husband. Were swindling, infamous forgers to be allowed with impunity to trifle with the Royal Majesty, and to pollute the most august names with their scandals and crimes? It was in vain that cautious politicians, like the Count of Vergennes, for example, tried to urge gentle measures; the Queen, impatient and angered, with the exaltation that gives to innocence the feeling of justice, of right, of honor, wished instantly to have truth given to the world.

It was August 15, 1785, Assumption Day; already the candles had been lit in the chapel of the Versailles palace; the courtiers were waiting in the Gallery of the Mirrors for the King and Queen to issue from their apartments, to go to mass. In the midst of this brilliant throng was the Cardinal de Rohan, who was about to officiate in his capacity of Grand Almoner, and was already wearing his pontifical robes. It was about midday. Suddenly the Cardinal was summoned to the King's room. Louis XVI., Marie Antoinette, the Baron de Breteuil, Keeper of the Seals and Minister of Foreign Affairs, were all there.

The King, when he saw the Cardinal approach him, asked him:—

"Have you bought any diamonds of Boehmer?"

"Yes, Sire."

"What have you done with them?"

"I thought that they had been delivered to the Queen."

"Who entrusted this business to you?"

"A lady named the Countess de La Motte-Valois, who gave me a letter from the Queen, and I thought to pay my court to the Queen by taking charge of this business."

Then Marie Antoinette broke out:—

"What, sir, could you think that I, who have not spoken to you for eight years, could have chosen you for this business, and through a woman like her?"

The Cardinal answered:—

"I see that I have been cruelly deceived; I will pay for the necklace. My desire to please Your Majesty blinded me; I did not detect any trickery, and I am sorry for it."

Then he drew from his pocket a notebook whence he took out the alleged letter from the Queen to Madame de La Motte. He looked at Marie Antoinette, fancying that he was about to crush her. But what was not his amazement when Louis XVI., having glanced at the letter, said:—

"That is not the Queen's writing or the Queen's signature. How could a prince of the house of Rohan, a Grand Almoner, have imagined that the

Queen signed 'Marie Antoinette of France'? Everybody knows that queens sign only with their baptismal names."

This remark was a revelation to the guilty and unhappy Cardinal. He was already turning pale when the King showed him a copy of a letter he had written to the jeweller.

"Sir," then said Louis XVI., "have you written a letter like this?"

"I do not remember writing it."

"And if you should be shown the original signed by you?"

"If the letter has my signature, it is genuine."

"Explain this whole mystery; I do not want to find you guilty, I desire your justification. Tell me what is the meaning of all this affair with Boehmer,—these promises and notes."

The Cardinal, in his emotion, could scarcely stand. Leaning, to support himself, against a table, he stammered, "Sire, I am too much agitated to answer Your Majesty in a proper—"

"Control yourself, Cardinal, and go into my study; there you will find paper, pens, and ink; put down what you have to say in writing."

The Cardinal went into the King's study and dashed off a few lines.

The Queen afterwards stated that she then was seized by a great panic, imagining that possibly the Cardinal, in order to ruin her, had set a horrible snare. Perhaps he was going to maintain that she had received the necklace and was about to mention some secret spot in the palace where some accomplice had concealed it. This fear was groundless. In a few minutes the Cardinal came back; his written defence no clearer, no more satisfactory than had been his oral explanations. Then Louis XVI. said to him, "Withdraw, sir."

The Cardinal at once left the King's room, and re-entered the Gallery of the Mirrors. The courtiers did not know what had happened, and imagined that he was going to the chapel. He had acquired control over his face which betrayed no agitation. It is easy to conceive the general emotion when suddenly the Baron de Breteuil was seen to turn to an ensign of the body-guard and heard to say, "Arrest the Cardinal de Rohan." It was like a thunderbolt.

The prelate could not look forward without terror to the fate that awaited him if the letters which he had received from Madame de La Motte should fall into the hands of justice. These letters were in Paris, at his palace, rue Vieille du Temple, in a little red letter-case. At the very moment of the catastrophe he showed great presence of mind: The young ensign who had been ordered to arrest him, preserved a respectful attitude. The Cardinal, who had just left the Gallery of the Mirrors, saw his servant at the door of the drawing-room of Hercules, and he said to him a few words in German. Then he asked the ensign for a lead-pencil. The officer at once gave him one which he had in his pocket. The

Cardinal wrote a few lines on a scrap of paper, which he gave to his man. A moment later the man mounted his horse and dashed away at full speed, reaching the palace in a very short time; there he burned all the letters in the red portfolio. Soon the lieutenant of police arrived, but it was too late.

Nevertheless, the Cardinal was locked up in the Bastille, where he was received by the governor, one of his friends. Louis XVI., who was always good-nature itself, had said, speaking of the new prisoner, "I do not wish his ruin, but in his own interest I must make sure of his person." At the Bastille, the Cardinal was lodged in the apartment of the King's lieutenant. He was at liberty to see his counsel and his relatives, and whenever he desired, to walk in the governor's garden. He had two valets de chambre at his orders. According to the Abbé Georgel, his table was served as became his birth and position. All the officials were eager to diminish for him the discomforts of captivity; but his heart, tortured more by spite than by remorse, was the prey of the liveliest fear and anguish.

What had become of Madame de La Motte meanwhile? August 17 she was supping two leagues from Bar-sur-Aube, in the famous Abbey of Clairvaux, where great preparations were making for the festival of Saint Bernard, August 20. This year it was the Abbé Maury, later well known for his success in the tribune, who was to pronounce the panegyric on the saint. At that time the superior of the Abbey was a man of great elegance, Dom Rocourt, who had an income of three or four hundred thousand francs and never travelled except in a carriage with four horses, and an outrider in front. Dom Rocourt knew about the relations of the Cardinal de Rohan with Madame de La Motte; hence, says the Count Beugnot, he treated her "like a princess of the Church."

They were awaiting the arrival of the Abbé Maury before sitting down to table. Nine o'clock had just struck, but he had not come, and they had decided to sup without him; but hardly had they taken their places when the sound of carriage wheels was heard. It was the Abbé Maury. Dom Rocourt went to greet him and made him sit down at table at once. Then he was asked what was the news in Paris.

"The news," he answered, "you ask? There's a piece of news which no one understands, which puzzles all Paris. The Cardinal de Rohan was arrested last Tuesday, Assumption Day, in his pontifical robes, on leaving the King's study. Does any one know why? No, not exactly. Something has been said about a diamond necklace which he was to have bought for the Queen and did not buy. It is inconceivable that for such a trifle the Grand Almoner of France should have been arrested in his pontifical robes, — you understand, in his pontifical robes, — on leaving the King's study."

When Madame de La Motte heard the Abbé Maury, she dropped her napkin and turned pale. She left the table, ordered a carriage, and set out at once for her house at Bar-sur-Aube. That night she burned all the letters she had received from the Cardinal. The next day, the 18th, she was arrested at five in the morning, at once carried to Paris and imprisoned in the Bastille. As yet there was no order for her husband's arrest. Five days later he was sought, but he had left Bar-sur-Aube, fleeing to England, where he could not be arrested.

Rétaux de Villette also fled to foreign parts, going to Geneva; but he was rash enough to walk in the neighborhood, on French territory, and there he was arrested and locked up in the Bastille with the rest.

As to the d'Oliva, whose presence was necessary for the examination, she sought refuge in Brussels, but the Versailles cabinet soon secured her extradition. She, too, was put in the Bastille, which held all the guilty persons except M. de La Motte. The trial could begin.

XI.

THE TRIAL.

AN incident like that of the necklace could only happen in a society where the monarchical principle had lost its strength and glory. It has been said with perfect truth that the very fact that there was a trial was a sign of the times. In the letters-patent of September 5, 1785, wherein Louis XVI. informed the Parliament of Paris of the affair, we find the words: "We have not been able to see without just indignation that an august name, dear to us in many ways, has been boldly taken, and that the respect due to the Royal Majesty has been violated with unheard-of insolence." Was it not strange that the Parliament should be called on to investigate whether the statements made by the King in public letters were true or false? How could the magistrates be asked to pass upon the King's assertions? Either there should have been no letters-patent of this sort, or there should have been no trial.

Before reaching this decision, Louis XVI. had proposed to the Cardinal to choose between casting himself on his clemency and being brought before the Parliament. The prelate discussed the plan he should adopt with his advocates, Target, Tronchet, Collet, and de Bonnières. Tronchet urged appealing to the royal clemency; Target, on the other hand, dissuaded his client from this course. This difference reminds us that one day Tronchet was boldly to defend Louis XVI., while Target declined this noble duty. Possibly the advocates who urged a trial fancied that the Cardinal's acquittal would be a blow to the Queen. It will be well to notice the conduct during the debates before the Parliament of these men who formed, as it were, the advance line of the Revolution: d'Esprémènil, Fretteau, Robert de Saint Vincent, Hérault de Séchelles.

At first, the Cardinal had been wholly prostrated; but when he learned that his correspondence with Madame de La Motte — those absurd letters which would have overwhelmed him with ridicule and infamy — had been burned; when he saw the inconceivable movement of public opinion in his favor, which was due to hatred of the Queen; when he perceived the energetic measures of his intelligent grand vicar, the Abbé Georgel, — he became more confident, and decided not to appeal to the royal clemency, but to stand trial. Consequently, he wrote to the King: "Sire, I very respectfully thank Your Majesty for the alternative offered to me; I have no hesitation in preferring the Parliament as the surest means of unmasking the intrigue of which I am the victim, and of proving my good faith and innocence."

According to the old rules, the competent tribunal would have been an ecclesiastical court. But can one imagine a council of bishops passing judgment on a necklace, deciding a gross swindle, and pronouncing between a cardinal and a woman of doubtful reputation? Nevertheless, when the Pope learned that a prince of the Church was submitting himself to lay jurisdiction, he was deeply moved by this renunciation of ancient privilege, and summoned a consistory, which declared unanimously that the Cardinal de Rohan had sinned against his dignity as a member of the Holy College, by recognizing the authority of the Parliament, that he was suspended for six months, and that, if he persisted, his name should be stricken from the list of cardinals.

But the prelate had taken the precaution to insert a protest against lay jurisdiction in a petition to the Parliament. A doctor of the Sorbonne was sent to Rome, to carry to the Pope a copy of this document; and he persuaded his Holiness that if the Cardinal had, to his great regret, and despite his formal protest, accepted the jurisdiction of a lay tribunal, it was because he had been compelled to bow before the royal authority. The Vatican accepted this explanation, and the Prince of Rohan was restored to his rights and honors as Cardinal.

The Parliament, then, had jurisdiction in this matter. What imprudence, what a false move on the part of the government, to submit a case like this to an assembly already agitated by revolutionary feelings, to an ambitious body, full of rancor against the authority of the crown! What a revenge for this Parliament — persecuted, curbed, exiled by Louis XV. — to decide on the fame of his successor's wife! What a gratification for these limbs of the law to have to judge between a queen and a prince of the Church! With what rapture these gallant magistrates — more interested in Venus than in Themis, to use the language of that time — would enjoy the importunities and solicitations of the prettiest women in Paris, of the great ladies related or connected by interest with the great house of Rohan!

The revolutionary feeling was not mistaken; the affair was a huge scandal, and a possibly irreparable onslaught against the principle of authority. Consequently, public opinion was aroused about this drama which suited so well the tastes and instincts of the time. All classes of society were interested. The nobility could not comprehend that a Rohan, innocent or guilty, should be accused. All the ecclesiastics, from the humblest abbé to the archbishops and cardinals, refused to admit that a prince of the Church could be submitted to secular jurisdiction. The philosophers delighted to see a queen contesting with a cardinal. The magistrates were puffed up with their own importance; the advocates were delighted to publish papers which were printed in vast numbers and made the reputation of their authors. The idlers and the gossips — and Heaven knows if there is any lack of them in a city like Paris — were amused beyond measure at this legal entertainment which fed the public curiosity and love of scandal. For nine months this strange affair of the necklace was the subject of perpetual discussion in the court and the city. The suburbs, too, took part, and demagogues yet unknown gave lessons in hatred and contempt.

Curiously enough, the scandals in the life of the Cardinal de Rohan seemed perfectly natural to his contemporaries. He was looked upon as a gentleman of distinguished gallantry. His appointment to the post of Grand Almoner of France seemed most natural and appropriate. This society, with all its democratic tendencies, was still infatuated with titles and coat-of-arms. The Cardinal was admired for his extravagance, his noble bearing, his grand air. It never occurred to any one to blame him for having contributed to Madame de La Motte's support out of his revenues as Grand Almoner. No one blamed him for consorting with charlatans, swindlers, and demireps. These things did not prevent his being looked on as a virtuous and sensible man, to use the language of that time. Every one sympathized with him; it was the fashion in high society to wear red and yellow ribbons, the color of "the Cardinal on the straw."

There were people ready to condemn Marie Antoinette, who believed, or pretended to believe, that after obstinately refusing the necklace when her husband offered it to her, she had had it given to her by

Madame de La Motte and the Cardinal de Rohan; that she had arranged the whole matter as a snare for the Cardinal, whose lack of favor was notorious. There were people credulous or malicious enough to maintain that the Queen of France could be seduced by a gift of jewelry, and that she gave assignations at night in the park of Versailles. To whom? To the Grand Almoner, a priest fifty years old. But calumny halts at nothing; hate never reasons; when men's fancies are so foul and such gross fables find currency, we may be sure that the Revolution was not far off.

The affair of the necklace, serious and fatal as it was, was yet treated almost derisively. One might have said that the only desire of the advocates was to distract and amuse the public; they indulged in the most grotesque extravagances. Maitre Doitot, Madame de La Motte's advocate, led off with a pamphlet, "the wildest that ever fell from a lawyer's pen; it was no less successful because it was the preface of the thousand and one nights and it was the work of an old fellow of seventy," (Memoirs of the Count of Beugnot). The memorial drawn up for Cagliostro by Maitre Thilorier was even more successful. The house of this famous worker of wonders was besieged by a multitude eager to buy this singular production, and it was necessary 'to post guards at the door. Maitre Thilorier spoke about the subterraneous galleries of Memphis, whence his hero had issued; of the labyrinth of the Pyramids, where he had been brought up; of his career of mysteries and miracles. The advocate, who was an intelligent man, was the first to laugh at this ridiculous story; but the public deemed it just and proper.

Maitre Polverit had charge of the defence of Cagliostro's wife, Serafina Feliciani. In his memorial, a masterpiece of bombast, he said of his client: "Endowed with a beauty such as no other woman possesses, she is not a model of tenderness, gentleness, and resignation; no, for she does not even suspect the existence of the opposite faults: her character offers to us poor human beings the ideal of a perfection which we may adore, but which we cannot comprehend." As to the memorial drawn up in the name of the d'Oliva, "it touched every tender heart," says the Abbé Georgel, "by the frankness of her confessions. Its style had the fresh coloring which poets attribute to the Queen of Cnidius and Paphos." What made the young woman still more interesting was, that she gave birth to a child in the Bastille, which she nursed herself.

Meanwhile, the Abbé Georgel was preparing his patron's defence with equal zeal and intelligence. He gave directions to the lawyers, brought influence to bear on the judges, set every secret spring in motion. Every day he wore out six horses in hurrying from one place to another. He slept every night only three or four hours. With the aid of two secretaries, he managed everything, took charge of the Cardinal's affairs, bringing them into order, reducing his extravagant expenditures in his palace at Saverne and in his mansion at Paris, satisfying Boehmer and Bassenge, and securing their payment by means of instalments from the revenues of the Abbey of Saint Waast.

The Abbé Georgel as Grand Vicar especially exulted in his power of giving spiritual comfort. In one of his epistles, Saint Paul, who was in captivity, exhorts his disciple, Saint Timothy, not to be ashamed of his prison and to give in his name the bread of the word to the faithful. The Abbé Georgel, in the absence of the Cardinal de Rohan, having to prepare the charge for Lent in 1786, judged it necessary to begin with quoting from this epistle. "The charge which was very successful," said the Grand Vicar, "was nothing but a happy combination of texts from Holy Writ, arranged to suit the circumstances." It was posted on the doors and sacristies of the chapel in the palace at Versailles, of the Blind Asylum, and of the Convent of the Nuns of the Assumption in Paris; but this was regarded as an improper proceeding. Louis XVI. was assured that by comparing the prisoner of the Bastille to Saint Paul, the Abbé Georgel implied a comparison between his King and Nero, and the over-zealous Grand Vicar was sent to exile in the provinces.

The examination advanced slowly, and the public awaited the results with eager curiosity. The Prince of Condé, who had married a princess of the house of Rohan, the Marshal of Soubise and the Countess of

Marsan, who both belonged to this family, spared no pains to save the Cardinal.

M. Pierre de Laurencel, the substitute of the Attorney-General, sent to the Queen a list of names of members of the High Court of Justice, with a statement of the means employed by the Cardinal's friends to secure their votes in the trial. "I had charge of this list," says Madame Campan, "among the papers which the Queen entrusted to my father-in-law. I have burned it, but I remember that many women figured in it in a way that cast no credit on their morals. It was by them, and by the large sums of money which they had received, that the oldest and most venerable persons were bribed."

Still light gradually broke, and the perfect innocence of the Queen began to appear indisputable. Could the most prejudiced imagine for a moment that Marie Antoinette would have wished to buy secretly a necklace which could only have been agreeable to her if she wore it? And even supposing, against every probability, that she desired this jewel merely to lock it up among her jewels, was it possible to believe that she would have chosen to make the purchase, a bishop, the Grand Almoner, a man extremely distasteful to her, to whom she had not spoken for eight years? On the other hand, it was proved that she had never had the slightest relations with Madame de La Motte, and Rétaux de Villette confessed that he had written with his own hand on the contract between the Cardinal and the jewellers, the words: " Approved. Marie Antoinette de France."

With equal frankness, the d'Oliva disclosed the part she had played in the scene in the park. Finally, the Cardinal himself declared that he had been deceived, and reproached Madame de La Motte with all impostures of which she had been guilty. Her line of defence was inadmissible. "It is the Cardinal who stole the necklace," she said; "it was in accordance with his orders that my husband and I had the diamonds separated and sold. The luxury with which I am reproached and which is alleged to have come from the sale of the necklace is really the result of the benefits bestowed on me by my friends, and especially by the Cardinal."

No, the Prince de Rohan, the Grand Almoner of France, was not a rogue or a thief; he was a man of wild ambitions, a coxcomb deluded by an adventuress of rare audacity, skill, and charm. The enigma was made clear; the Cardinal had been the dupe of a huge deception. But one very serious fact remained equally clear: that the prelate had entered into relations with a worthless woman to buy a necklace for the Queen, against the King's wishes, and that his intrigues, his hopes, the part he played in the scene in the garden, were so many insults to the Queen's honor, to the royal dignity. "That was the crime," said Count Beugnot, "the crime for which respect for religion, for the Royal Majesty, and for morality, all of which had been outraged, demanded punishment." The trial lasted nine months, amid an excitement which grew from day to day; never had the public curiosity been so thoroughly aroused as on the day when the Parliament was to render the long-expected verdict.

XII.

THE VERDICT.

ALL Paris was in expectation, May 29, 1786, when the assembled Parliament was at last about to render its judgment. In the night between the 29th and the 30th, the prisoners were transferred from the Bastille to the Conciergerie. Who would have said that the moment when the illegitimate descendant of the Valois was entering this fatal place, that seven years later, the legitimate daughter of the German Cæsars, the Queen of France and Navarre, would also cross the threshold of this prison?

May 30, the Parliament opened its morning sitting, and the persons accused were introduced in turn. The first to appear was Madame de La Motte, who could not restrain a movement of horror on seeing the final preparations. Then she cast a bold glance upon the judges, and persisting in her plan of defence, she denied everything.

Then came the Cardinal's turn. The President, d'Aligre, had the stool of repentance removed. The Grand Almoner wore a long violet robe, the mourning dress of cardinals. His stockings and his cap were red. He wore his orders crosswise around his neck. Pale and serious, he entered with an air of dignity and sadness which impressed the judges, who were already well disposed towards him. Thrice the First President invited him most politely to be seated, and those of the judges who questioned him expressed marked sympathy and deference. When he said, "I was completely blinded by my intense desire to regain the Queen's good graces," every face showed thorough approval. When he had finished speaking, he arose and saluted the court as he withdrew. They all arose and returned his salute.

The deliberation was long and stormy. The judges were divided into two hostile camps: the defenders of the Queen, and her enemies. Her defenders wished some stigma to be placed upon the man who had dared to insult the Royal Majesty: the others had a very different aim; they demanded an acquittal, pure and simple, for the Cardinal, and thus, implicitly, a condemnation of Marie Antoinette.

The Attorney-General, Joly de Fleury, demanded the following verdict, so far as the Cardinal was concerned: —

"Louis René Edouard de Rohan is compelled to declare in court, in the presence of the Attorney-General, the High Court of Justice assembled, that it is without reason that he permitted himself to believe in a false and imaginary nocturnal interview on the terrace of Versailles;

"That it is rashly, ignorantly, and without assurance of the wishes of the King and the Queen, that he undertook and carried on negotiations with Boehmer and Bassenge concerning the purchase of the diamond necklace;

"That, after the necklace was given to him, he, by false and fabricated assertions, continued to encourage the aforesaid Boehmer and Bassenge in the belief of the genuineness of the purchase, and that, by his own confession, even after being convinced by examination that the 'approved' and the signature were false, he has, by continued misuse of the Queen's name, made to the aforesaid Boehmer and Bassenge, a payment of thirty thousand francs, of which he has taken a receipt in the Queen's name;

"That he repent and ask pardon of the King and Queen for having had the temerity to lack the respect due to their sacred persons;

"It is required that it be forbidden to the aforesaid de Rohan to approach the Royal palaces and all other places where the King and Queen may reside, until it shall please the King to order otherwise;

"It is ordered that in the term to be fixed by the court, the aforesaid de Rohan shall be compelled to resign the post and honor of Grand Almoner of France, with which the King has honored him;

"The aforesaid de Rohan is condemned to the payment of such sums to be bestowed in charity as shall please the court;

"It is ordered that the aforesaid de Rohan shall remain in prison until he shall have obeyed and satisfied the judgment which shall have been rendered."

This verdict would have been an act of respect for the Queen; but they were very far from being satisfactory to the princes and princesses of the house of Condé, with which the Cardinal was connected, or to the families of Rohan, Soubise, and Guéménée, the members of which had put on mourning, and in this gloomy attire lined the passages through which the members of the High Court had to pass. On the other hand, the revolutionary spirit desired simply to wound and distress the Queen. Fifteen judges adopted purely and simply the verdict of the Attorney-General; eight others favored the gentler opinion of the President d'Ormesson, who desired that the Cardinal should make full amends, but should keep his functions and honors. It may be truly said that this last opinion was moderation itself, yet to the enemies of Marie Antoinette it appeared too severe. Robert de Saint Vincent made a speech in which he condemned the publicity given to the trial, and denounced the King and Queen for not having a minister wise enough to save them from thus compromising the majesty of the throne. Finally, after deliberating eighteen hours, the Cardinal's friends carried the day by a majority of three.

May 31, 1786, at nine in the evening, the Parliament pronounced its judgment. The Cardinal and Cagliostro were acquitted purely and simply; M. de La Motte was condemned in default to the galleys for life, and Rétaux de Villette to banishment. In the same judgment the Parliament condemned Madame de La Motte "to be beaten, naked, with a rope round her neck; and to be branded with the letter V (*voleuse*) on the two shoulders by the public executioner; this done, to be carried to the House of Correction of the Salpêtrière, where she is to be detained and imprisoned for life." As for the d'Oliva, she was simply acquitted. The judgment furthermore declared that the word, "Approved," and the signature, "Marie Antoinette de France," falsely ascribed to the Queen, had been fraudulently placed on the margin of the writing entitled: "Propositions and Conditions concerning the Price and Mode of Payment of the Necklace."

There was not in the whole judgment a single word condemning the Cardinal; and no mention was made of his relations with Madame de La Motte or of the scene in the park. Count Beugnot says very justly in his Memoirs: "Even now, when the Revolution has only too far weakened the feeling of respect for the Royal Family, even now, who can imagine that the Parliament looked upon the scene in the garden of Versailles merely as a swindle and the participants as merely swindlers and their victim? The Revolution was already complete in the minds of those who could consider such an insult to the King, in the person of the Queen, with this culpable indifference and insolent composure."

At the moment when the verdict was rendered a

vast crowd was assembled in the neighborhood of the Palais de Justice, and uproarious applause broke forth at the news of his acquittal. When the judges were leaving the palace, the multitude kissed their hands and flung themselves on their knees, amid the most enthusiastic applause.

Applaud, ye calumniators of Marie Antoinette! You are only at the beginning of your career of hatred and savage joy. Other pleasures await you in the tribunes of the Jacobins and in those of the Convention, before the Conciergerie and at the foot of the scaffold!

The Cardinal received most enthusiastic ovations on his return to his house in the rue Vieille du Temple; but a few hours later he received from Louis XVI. the command to send back the ribbon of the Holy Ghost and to hand in his resignation of the post of Grand Almoner. Moreover, a *lettre de cachet* exiled him to his abbey of the Chaise-Dieu, in Auvergne. Yet, strange as it may seem, the Abbé Georgel was surprised, or feigned surprise, at this perfectly natural event. "Who could have imagined," he said in his Memoirs, "that so glorious a day could be followed by a day of disgrace and exile? Were we not justified in expecting that the King, in his delight at finding innocence where he had suspected guilt, would manifest his love of justice by bestowing on the Grand Almoner the highest marks of favor?" Could the Abbé Georgel have supposed that the Cardinal was to be appointed Prime Minister on the day after the verdict was given?

According to the Baron de Besenval, on the other hand, "every sensible person understood that the King was showing his aversion to the Cardinal who had dared so boldly and indecently to compromise the Queen; it was impossible that he should keep his place any longer, and as for his exile, he had well deserved it." Such was doubtless the opinion of reasonable people, but reasonable people were rare in Paris in 1786. The day of his departure, the Cardinal saw a vast multitude thronging the courtyards of his house and calling him to the windows; he appeared there and gave the crowd his episcopal blessing.

The Abbé Georgel, whose capacity for surprise is really extraordinary, could not understand that Marie Antoinette should not have been pleased with the verdict. "Is it credible," he exclaims, "that the news of the Cardinal's triumph had to be broken to the Queen very gently? No one wished to announce the result to her. Her dearest friend, the Duchess of Polignac, was induced to tell her." Yes, Marie Antoinette had measured with a glance the abyss which calumny and hate were opening before her; she perceived how far the treachery and malice of her enemies would go. "Come," she said to Madame Campan, "come, pity your insulted Queen, the victim of intrigues and injustice. But I, for my part, will pity you as a Frenchwoman. If I, in a matter which concerned my character, failed to find upright judges, what can you expect if you should have a law case in which your fortune and your fame were at stake?"

Weber records that it was on this occasion, in speaking of the infamous calumnies of which she began to be the object, that Marie Antoinette uttered these admirable words, so worthy of her noble heart: "It seems as if malice had coolly devised every possible way of wounding me; but I shall triumph over my enemies by trebling the good I have tried to do; it is easier for certain people to distress me, than to compel me to revenge myself."

What was the fate of the different persons who figured in this affair of the necklace? Louis XVI. treated the Cardinal with no excess of severity; the prelate, finding that the Abbey of the Chaise-Dieu, among the mountains of Auvergne, was an unfavorable place for his health, received permission from the King to reside at his Abbey of Marmoutier, near Tours. Soon afterwards, he was allowed to return to Strasburg, where he resumed the direction of his diocese. When the Revolution broke out, he withdrew to that part of his bishopric which lay on the other side of the Rhine. His noble conduct, his generous aid to the émigrés, a marked improvement in his morals, compensated for his past misdeeds, and his long scandalous life came to a Christian end: he died peacefully at Ettenheim, February 16, 1803.

Cagliostro, on the day after he left the Bastille, received orders to leave France without delay. He went to England, and afterwards to Switzerland and

Italy. This singular character, who, after all, was no ordinary man, — this philanthropic magician, who, with all his frauds, had yet a fascinating side, and humored the omnipresent taste for the supernatural, — ended his singular and eventful life in sad circumstances. He was arrested in Rome, in 1789, as a Freemason, and condemned to death by the Inquisition; this sentence having been commuted to imprisonment for life, he was confined in the Castle of Saint Leon, and there he died in 1795.

The d'Oliva, whose fame was magnified by the affair of the necklace, received many proposals of marriage. She chose for her husband one of her former lovers, a certain Beausire, who, a few years later, had the honor of being guillotined, along with many noble victims, in the Revolution.

As for Madame de La Motte, everything in this wretched woman's career was horrible and violent; she was more deeply marked by fatality than by the branding-iron of the executioner. She was sentenced to be shaved, stripped, and beaten, and to be branded on her shoulders with a red-hot iron — an indelible sign of infamy. The details of the infliction of these penalties are most horrible. They took place June 21, 1786, in the courtyard of the Palais de Justice. The wretched woman struggled with all her might and main, so that she had to be carried to the scaffold. Even when she was loaded with chains she continued her struggles. Her piercing cries, her efforts to escape, only redoubled, and, in her writhing, the hot iron slipped from her shoulder to her breast. A last shriek, more terrible than the others, was heard, and the unhappy woman was driven to the Salpêtrière, her prison. She was unrecognizable — her face all bruises, her eyes swollen with tears — when, quivering with anger and despair, she crossed the threshold of this accursed spot. There she was the object of public curiosity: people came from all quarters of Paris to see her. It was forbidden to speak to her, but she could be seen in the prison courtyard, and was easily distinguished from among her fallen companions by her air of misery and her continual lamentations. One night in September, 1787, she found a means of escaping, and found refuge in England, where she lived on hate and calumny. Her vile pamphlets anticipated the shameless denunciations of the bloodthirsty women who sat knitting at the foot of the guillotine, and, like a venomous serpent, she sought to poison the Queen with her venom.

Hired libellers carried on the campaign of lies. Even Michelet, the open enemy of thrones, has thus condemned them: "Hired by the Queen's enemies, they composed about Marie Antoinette, in a few pages, a horrible legend, which was absurd, foolish, and disgusting, according to which she was both a Messalina and a la Brinvilliers, poisoning every one who stood in her way, giving arsenic to every newcomer." The end of Madame de La Motte was no less tragic than her whole career. One evening, in

1791, she imagined that she was pursued by men who wanted to arrest her and carry her back to the Salpêtrière. Wild with terror, she jumped out of the window. She was not instantly killed; but one thigh was broken in two places, her left arm was fractured, one eye was lost; and she lingered for three weeks. Thus disappeared the last of the Valois.

The more we study the beginning and the results of the affair of the necklace, the more odious and tragic it appears. One man was particularly struck by it, and the moment it began, he had a prophetic insight of the terrible consequences which were to ensue. This man, who was in Strasburg in 1770, when Marie Antoinette arrived in France, had been shocked by seeing in the pavilion by which the Princess entered the island of the Rhine, tapestry representing the story of Jason, Medea, and Creüsa; that is to say, the picture of the most unhappy of marriages. He was not mistaken when he shuddered at this evil omen, nor was he mistaken when the first news of the affair of the necklace reached him. "In 1785," he wrote in his *Annalen, oder Tag- und Jahreshefte, 1749–1822*, "the affair of the necklace produced an indefinable impression upon me. From this abyss of immorality, which, in the town, the court, and throughout the whole state, opened before me, I saw rising the most terrible consequences, and for a long time I could not free my imagination from the ghosts that haunted it. Once in particular I spoke about this incident with so much emotion that my friends with whom I was staying in the country when the first news came, confided to me later, long after the outbreak of the Revolution, that I seemed to them out of my head." This man, whose presentiments were so accurate, was both a great prophet and a great poet; it was Goethe.

October 14, 1793, Marie Antoinette appeared before the Revolutionary tribunal. The public prosecutor, who called her Frédégonde, Medicis, Messalina, Brunehaut, did not linger over the affair of the necklace; there was but a brief exchange of questions and answers: "Did you know the woman La Motte?" "I never saw her." "Was she not your victim in the affair of the necklace?" "She could not have been, for I never saw her." That was all; not another word. Why did not Fouquier-Tinville press the point? Because he confessed by his silence that the only guilty person was Madame de La Motte.

Now there is no longer any obscurity; eminent historians, who certainly cannot be accused of reactionary tendencies or of any partiality for monarchies, M. Henri Martin and M. Lavallée, for example, have rendered full justice to the Queen who was so infamously attacked. The first named has said, "The conviction which results from this long and confused affair is the impossibility of the Queen's guilt." "There is no doubt that Marie Antoinette was innocent," says the other; yet, in spite of the testimony

f the facts, still there are possibly people, who, more
unjust to the royal martyr than even Fouquier-Tinville, will try to collect in pamphlets as absurd as
base, gall and mire wherewith to sully a pure and
venerable name.

XIII.

A PICTURE OF MADAME LEBRUN'S.

VISITORS of the portrait-gallery in the palace of Versailles, always stop before one picture, which has a charm and beauty that are sure to attract attention. It is that in which Madame Vigée-Lebrun, in 1787, painted Marie Antoinette, surrounded by her three children. The Queen is sitting in the drawing-room of Peace, close to the Gallery of the Mirrors; on her head she wears a velvet cap surmounted by a tuft of white feathers. Her red velvet dress, bordered with sable, shows her foot resting on a cushion. The Queen's complexion is marvellously brilliant, but her expression, while both gentle and full of majesty, has a dreamy, melancholy air. On her right stands a little girl, eight or nine years old, leaning her head on her mother's shoulder, and holding her arm. This child is Marie Thérèse Charlotte, the future Duchess of Angoulême. On her knees Marie Antoinette is holding a two-year-old child, — Louis Charles of France, the Duke of Normandy, who later was to call himself Louis XVII. On the left is an empty cradle, the covering of which is upheld by a child of six. This child wears the blue ribbon and the insignia of the Holy Ghost; it is the Dauphin.

The Queen's sad expression is easily explained: Marie Antoinette had just lost her second daughter, Sophie Beatrix, who died when a year old, and this sad death, coinciding with the outbreak of calumny and the first threatening of the Revolutionary storm, was for the unhappy mother's tender heart a great sorrow and an unhappy omen. June 25, 1787, Madame Elisabeth wrote to her friend, the Marchioness of Bombelles: "Your relatives will have told you that Sophie died the day after I wrote to you. . . . My niece [later the Duchess of Angoulême] has been most admirable; she showed a tenderness uncommon at her age. Her poor little sister is very fortunate. She has escaped all dangers. I, in my idleness, regret that I did not share her lot in my childhood. To console myself, I tended her carefully, hoping that she would pray for me. I count much on that. If you only knew how pretty she was when she lay dying! It is inconceivable. The night before, she was pink and white, not at all emaciated; indeed, most lovely."

The little Princess had been conceived at the moment when the trial of the necklace began. She was the last comer, the pledge of a conjugal harmony which calumniators and evil tongues had not been able to disturb, in spite of every invention of malice. Her death was the prelude of the afflictions of every sort that were about to fall upon the unhappy Marie Antoinette.

One who looks at Madame Lebrun's picture will be struck by the general melancholy expressed upon the canvas, in spite of the splendor of the dresses and the rich coloring. The sadness of the oldest girl, with her eyes raised to heaven, the precocious seriousness of the Dauphin, the gesture with which he points towards his brother, afterwards Louis XVII., the pensive, thoughtful attitude of Marie Antoinette, who seems to be dreaming about the lamentable future fate of her children, seem to be a presentiment of the artist. There is a smile on the lips of the Duke of Normandy, because he is at an age when mental suffering is yet unknown. This pathetic picture, in spite of all its splendor, recalls the children of Charles I., painted by Van Dyke.

Madame Lebrun finished her picture in 1787, meaning to send it to the exhibition at the Louvre in 1788. "The frame was first taken there alone," she writes in her Memoirs, "and this fact was enough to call forth abundant abuse. 'There is the Deficit,' people said, as well as a great many other things which were repeated to me, and enabled me to foresee the severest criticism. At last I sent the picture, but I was afraid to follow it and see its fate, so much did I dread the adverse judgment of the public. Indeed, I was so uneasy that I actually became feverish. I went to my room and locked the door, and was praying that my picture of the royal family might succeed, when my brother and a number of friends came to tell me that I had made a public success."

It has been asserted that in 1788 the feeling of the public about Marie Antoinette was so abominably unjust that the government had hesitated, in the first days of the exhibition of the Louvre, about exposing Madame Lebrun's picture. But it is certain that the sympathetic artist's eloquent brush silenced malice and disarmed criticism.

"After the Salon," continues Madame Lebrun, "the King having had my picture carried to Versailles, it was M. d'Angevilliers, then Minister of Fine Arts and Director of the Royal Buildings, who presented me to His Majesty. Louis XVI. was kind enough to talk with me for some time, and to tell me that he was satisfied; then he added, looking at my picture, 'I am not familiar with painting, but you make me love it.'"

The picture was placed in a hall of the grand apartments, through which the Queen passed every day on her way to and from mass. A day came when she no longer could endure to look at it. June 4, 1789, just at the opening of the States-General, so fatal to the monarchy, the Dauphin, a charming boy, amiable and intelligent, died at Meudon, in his eighth year. His poor mother, overwhelmed with grief, was unable to look at the canvas on which were the features of the dear boy for whose death she was weeping. She could never pass through the hall where this picture hung, without shedding tears, and a queen has no right to weep. "She told M. d'Angevilliers at that time," adds Madame Lebrun, "to have the picture taken away; but with her usual consideration she took care to have me informed at once, at the same time telling me the reason. It is to this thoughtfulness of the Queen that I owe the preservation of my picture; for the fishwomen and ruffians who soon after went to Versailles to secure Their Majesties, would certainly have destroyed it, as they did the Queen's bed, which they cut through and through."

By his brother's death, the future Louis XVII. became Dauphin. At the moment of his birth, this child, who was destined to so gloomy an end, was thought to have been born under a lucky star. His birthday was Easter Sunday, 1785, March 27. In opposition to the old custom, which postponed the baptism of the royal children for some years, the young Prince had been baptized that same evening, at eight o'clock, in the chapel of the palace at Versailles, by the Cardinal de Rohan, Grand Almoner of France. His godfather was his uncle, the future Louis XVIII.; his godmother, his aunt, the Queen of Naples, represented by Madame Elisabeth. The King, accompanied by all the court, had gone to the chapel, to be present at the baptism and the "Te Deum." When the ceremony was over, M. de Calonne, the Comptroller-General of Finance and Grand Treasurer of the Royal Orders, had carried to the infant the ribbon and star of the Order of the Holy Ghost. At nine o'clock there were fireworks before an interested crowd in the Place d'Armes. On the 24th of the following

May, Marie Antoinette came to Paris in great pomp to give thanks for her recovery. Fifty men of the body-guard and a brilliant suite accompanied her state carriage, which was drawn by eight horses. The cannon of the Invalides fired a salute, for the future martyr was still applauded. She went to Notre Dame; then to Saint Geneviève; and afterwards to the Tuileries, where she dined. The same evening she supped at the Temple, which she was to see again a few years later. The festivities ended with fireworks, which the Count of Aranda had set off from the roof of his house in the Place Louis XV. The Temple and the Place Louis XV.! Those words call up many memories.

On his birth, the prince received the title of Duke of Normandy, which had not been borne by any one since the fourth son of Charles IV. June, 1786, Louis XVI., on his way back from Cherbourg, where he had been visiting the great works he had commanded at this port, was warmly greeted by all Normandy. He congratulated himself on having given the name of his beautiful province to his second son. "Come, my little Norman," he said to him, as he took him in his arms, "your name will bring you good luck." At that time, everything seemed to smile on the son of the King of France.

When his brother died, Louis XVII. was but four years old. He was a remarkably handsome child. His blue eyes, his clear complexion, his curling light hair, made him look like an angel. He was also amiable, attractive, and more sensitive than most children of his age. One evening, at Saint Cloud, his mother sang and played to him a little song of Berquin's, and the young Prince, who was listening, did not move. "Hush! he's asleep," said Madame Elisabeth. But the child raised his head, and said eagerly, "Oh! dear aunt, can one sleep when Mamma Queen is singing?" He was taught to read in a book of the Marquis of Pompignan, which was a eulogy of the older brother of Louis XVI., the Duke of Burgundy, who died at nine, having endured intense suffering with surprising courage.

Louis XVI. had learned English by translating a Life of Charles I.; Louis XVII. learned to read in a book devoted to the memory of a child who endured much suffering. "How did my uncle learn," he asked, "to be so brave?"—a question which moved all who heard it. What would they have felt if they could have foreseen the cruel blows of fate, and if, in the dim future, they had suddenly descried the cobbler, Simon, like a spectre?

XIV.

MADAME ELISABETH AT MONTREUIL.

JUST when a thunder-storm is about to begin, the reader may have noticed a bird seeking refuge under the branches of a tree which the lightning threatens; this dove is like the young royal maiden, who, when the Revolution broke out, was living calmly and happily at Montreuil, an angel of innocence and virtue, whose mere name is a symbol of holiness, — Madame Elisabeth. Before the thunder begins to mutter and the lightning to flash, let us rest our eyes for a moment on this noble and worthy girl, soon to be a martyr; on this spotless lamb, one of the most touching victims of the Revolution. The time is approaching when Marie Antoinette will find herself abandoned by nearly all her defenders, her relatives, her servants. Even the women whom she had most honored with her friendship will leave her, either of their own choice, or in obedience to the demands of the multitude. But there is one woman who will not abandon her, one woman whose heroism will grow with the danger, who will remain full of devotion, even to death; this woman is the worthy sister of Louis XVI., the worthy descendant of Saint Louis.

In all history there are few figures so sympathetic, so gentle; few heads that wear so pure and bright a crown of glory. Are not such beings a sort of compensation for the evil, an expiation of crime in times of horror? One thinks with emotion of the holy women who wept at the Redeemer's sufferings on Golgotha, when the executioners, full of rage, were insulting Christ upon the cross; when the men of the Terror were filling France with tears and blood, we regard Madame Elisabeth, and the sight of this holy victim reconciles us with humanity.

The future martyr had known sorrow from the cradle. She was born May 3, 1764, and before she was three, had lost both father and mother. She transferred her affection to her brothers, and especially to the eldest, the Duke of Berry, later Louis XVI. The young Princess's education was confided to two women of superior worth, — the Countess of Marsan and the Baroness of Mackau. She was naturally enthusiastic, quick-tempered, and inclined to haughtiness; she became kind, gentle, humble. Religion so softened and modified her character that she became a saint. Her genuine piety was not at all severe; her devoutness was the expression of a noble soul in full light. Her conscience was as calm and clear as her face. She liked to pray with the young girls of Saint Cyr, or with the Carmelite Sisters of Saint Denis, among whom was her aunt, Madame

Louise de France, in religion, Mother Thérèse of Saint Augustine.

"Not satisfied with coming often to be edified with her aunt's virtues," writes one of the Carmelites, "she devoted herself to the humblest functions of a convent life. One day when she had arrived at an early hour at the nunnery, she expressed a desire to serve the dinner to the whole sisterhood; our revered Mother suggested to her this exercise, which suited her perfectly. She went into the refectory, put on an apron, and after kissing the earth, went to the kitchen door; she was given a tray on which was set the sisters' food. She distributed it to them carefully, when suddenly the tray tipped, and some of the food fell on the floor. Her embarrassment was intense; to relieve her, the Prioress said, 'My niece, after a blunder like that you should kiss the earth.' At once Madame Elisabeth prostrated herself, and then continued her task without further incident. It was a real pleasure to our venerable Mother to see the virtues of her family reappearing in this young princess." The sister of Louis XVI., serving the meal of the Carmelites along with the daughter of Louis XV., is a subject to be recommended to artists fond of painting religious pictures.

Many princes thought of asking for the hand of Madame Elisabeth. It is only necessary to glance at Sicardi's miniature, which belongs to the Marquis of Raigecourt, or at the lovely bust in the palace of Versailles, to understand the charm of this young and attractive princess. Then came up the question of her marriage with a prince of Portugal, and again, with Joseph II., who paid her much attention when he visited France in 1777. Political reasons prevented these proposed alliances, much to Madame Elisabeth's content.

Like Isabelle of France, the sister of Saint Louis, Madame Elisabeth preferred the happiness of remaining with a brother whom she loved, to an exile however brilliant. She was extremely fond of the palace of Versailles, where she was born; of its park full of reminiscences of her childhood, of the chapel where she had so often prayed. She had a sincere affection for her brothers, her aunts, her governesses, her maids of honor, and for her friends. Her tender soul would have been tortured by the thought of leaving them; hence she soon gave up all idea of marrying.

At an entertainment given at the Trianon, June 6, 1782, in honor of the Grand Duke Paul of Russia, the Baroness d'Oberkirch was given a place by the side of Madame Elisabeth. The Baroness in her Memoirs thus speaks of the Princess: "She was in all the glow of youth and beauty, and refused every offer, in order to remain with her family. 'I can marry only the son of a king, and the son of a king will have to reign over his father's realm; I should cease to be a Frenchwoman, and that I should not like. I prefer staying here at the foot of my brother's, to ascending any other throne.'"

When she came of age in 1778, Madame Elisabeth

wanted to keep all her masters. The Abbé of Montaigu, who has been compared with Fénelon for eloquence and gentleness, had directed her early studies. She was almost as devoted to work as to prayer.

In 1781, Louis XVI., who dearly loved his sister, made her a fitting present. At No. 41 of the Avenue de Paris, at Versailles, there is a little street running north and south, called the rue du Bon Conseil. At No. 2 in this street is the entrance into a building which extends for some distance along the Avenue de Paris. This house was built about 1776, for the governess of the royal children, the Princess of Rohan-Guéménée. A lovely garden was laid out there; from the top of a hillock, eight or ten metres high, which was ascended by a spiral staircase concealed in the shrubbery, there was a distant view of Paris, lying like a giant on the horizon. This pretty place was situated in what was then a suburb of Versailles, and was called Montreuil. In 1781, the Prince of Guéménée became bankrupt, and the Princess, in order to satisfy as far as possible, her husband's creditors, sold her diamonds, her furniture and estates, including the house and park of Montreuil. Madame Elisabeth had often walked there, and she greatly admired its shade and its flowers.

In spite of her love of solitude, she was the only princess of the royal family who had no country-house. One day in 1781, Marie Antoinette and Madame Elisabeth were driving along the Avenue de Paris. "If you like," said the Queen to her young sister-in-law, we will stop at that house in Montreuil, where you used to like to go when you were a little girl." "I shall be delighted," answered Madame Elisabeth; "for I have spent many happy hours there." The Queen and the Princess got out of their carriage, and just as they were crossing the threshold, Marie Antoinette said, "Sister, you are now in your own house. This is to be your Trianon. The King has the pleasure of offering this present to you, and has given me the happiness of informing you."

Madame Elisabeth was then but seventeen years old. The King decided that she should not sleep at Montreuil until she was twenty-five.

"But as soon as she came into the possession of her dear little estate, she spent only the evenings and the nights at Versailles. In the morning she would go to mass in the chapel of the palace, and then she would at once get into a carriage with one of her ladies to drive to Montreuil. Sometimes she would even walk there. The life she led there was monotonous and like that of the happiest family in a castle a hundred leagues from Paris. The hours for work, for exercise, for reading, in solitude or in company, were carefully appointed. The dinner hour brought the Princess and her ladies together at the same table," M. de Beauchesne tells us in his life of Madame Elisabeth.

In the same book he adds: "Later, before returning to court, they would all kneel down in the drawing-room, and in conformity to the habit surviving in some families, would have evening prayers together. Then they would return to the busy palace, at once so near and so remote, and enter their official home with the memory of a happy day filled with work, lightened by friendship, and consecrated by prayer."

The first thing that Madame Elisabeth did with her new property was to give to Madame de Mackau a little house adjacent, upon the estate. She thought that the best way of inaugurating her taking possession was by sharing it with her former instructress. The Baroness of Mackau, who was not rich, accepted gratefully the gift of the Princess, and established herself at Montreuil with her daughter, Madame de Bombelles, whom Madame Elisabeth treated like an old friend.

No one understood better than the sister of Louis XVI. the holy pleasures and exquisite charm of friendship. She was the benefactress of her two dearest companions, Mademoiselle de Causans and Mademoiselle de Mackau, who had become respectively the Marchioness of Raigecourt and the Marchioness of Bombelles; and Madame Elisabeth was grateful to both for the benefits she had conferred upon them; for truly high-minded people feel gratitude to those to whom they are able to be of service. To make a dowry for Mademoiselle de Causans, the Princess had advanced to her the allowance she would have received for five years, thirty thousand francs a year, from the King. With this sum of one hundred and fifty thousand francs Mademoiselle de Causans, who married the Marquis of Raigecourt, was able to remain near her benefactress. Louis XVI. signed the marriage contract June 27, 1784, and when every year anything was said about her allowance, Madame Elisabeth would say, "There is none for me; but then I have my Raigecourt."

Mademoiselle de Mackau, Marchioness of Bombelles, was two years older than the Princess, whose playmate she had been in childhood. On her marriage, in 1778, the King gave her a dowry of one hundred thousand francs, a pension of six thousand francs, and the position of companion to Madame Elisabeth. The Princess said: "At last my wishes are gratified; you are mine. How pleasant it is to think that there is a new tie between us, and to hope that nothing will loosen it!" M. de Bombelles was an officer; in 1785 he entered the diplomatic career, and in 1786 was the French minister at Lisbon. After losing his wife in 1800, he took orders, and became Bishop of Amiens in 1819. His third son, who entered the Austrian service, in 1834, married Marie Louise, the widow of Napoleon I.

M. Feuillet de Conches has published some of the letters written by Madame Elisabeth to her friends. Undoubtedly the sister of Louis XVI. would have been astonished if she had been told that some day her letters would be printed; for never was there a correspondence more void of literary pretensions. "Madame Elisabeth's style," says her editor, "is a real rough diamond, at once diffuse, familiar, and incorrect, simple and strong, natural and easy, a curious mixture of frankness, good sense, and strength, of original simplicity and the merriment of a school-girl, yet preserving all the flavor and tone of an old language, in its ease, while showing an intimate and tender playfulness which endears the writer to us."

The correspondence is full of pious and exalted thoughts. One might say that the sister of Louis XVI. already foresaw the approaching tempests, and was asking Heaven for strength to face them, with alarm. In many of the letters there is a sort of anticipation of her heroic endurance. It is easy to see that this young girl was no ordinary person; that deep in her heart lay hidden treasures of resignation, piety, and courage. Touching reflections, wise counsels, Christian meditations, abound especially in her letters to Madame Marie de Causans. She wrote to her, December 17, 1785: "How pleasant the idea of eternity becomes when we can say, 'I have spent all my life for God!'"

In 1786 Madame de Causans had just lost her mother; Madame Elisabeth tries to console her thus: "We must lay our fears and hopes at the foot of the cross; that alone can teach us to endure the trials that Heaven sends us. That is the book of books; it alone lifts up and consoles the afflicted soul. God was innocent, and suffered more than we can suffer, either in our heart or body. Ought we not to be happy to feel ourselves so closely bound to him who did so much for us? Life has cruel moments, but through them we attain a precious treasure. . . . Who knows how soon we may reach that moment, dreaded by many, and so longed for by your mother? Let us try to deserve that it be as calm and as exemplary." This wish of Madame Elisabeth's was granted; for no death can be more admirable, more sublime, than hers.

February 9, 1786, she wrote to Madame Marie de Causans: "Let us turn simply to God. May faith be given us to see that he never abandons his children! If we feel too weak for his service, if we are discouraged, let us not rely on ourselves alone; let us say to him: Thou, O God, seest all my heart; it is wholly thine. I do not know whether thou acceptest all the sacrifices which I make and intend; but thy Son died in atonement for my faults. Look upon him, O God, and even on the cross, where our cruelty and sins fastened him; hear him who intercedes for us, who consoled the penitent thief. I would imitate him, O God, and recognize thy sovereign power, and believe that, whatever may befall me, thou wilt not desert me." Madame Elisabeth ascended the scaffold; but as she climbed the steps, the God of mercy did not desert her, and death was rather an entrance into glory than a punishment.

She wrote to Madame de Causans, March 29, 1786: "Do not listen to the emptiness that surrounds you; and when it torments you too much, cast your eyes on Christ, and you will see that he has more sympathy and more care for you than you can expect from human beings. He is ever at your heart's door, asking only to enter." She wrote to Madame de Bombelles, July 2, 1787: "The more one sees of the world, the more dangerous it appears, or the more worthy of contempt rather than of regret when the time comes to leave it. Let us make ready for that moment." These preparations, so often neglected, were made most fully by this Princess.

In 1785 she witnessed the sudden death of one of the gardeners at Montreuil, and was with him when he received extreme unction. "Madame sets a noble example," said the attendant priest. "Sir," she replied, "I am receiving a greater one, and one that I shall never forget."

The continual thought of death, an unceasing contemplation of the crucifix, firm hope in a better world, formed the secret of Madame Elisabeth's strength. We feel that angels upheld her, and that the virtues made a sanctuary of her pure soul. The edifying death of her aunt, Madame Louise, the Carmelite, at Saint Denis, November 25, 1787, was for her a severe lesson; one that made her even more pious, more truly Christian. A moment before breathing her last the nun said, "It is time. . . . Come, rise, let us hasten to heaven." Madame Campan tells us that in her delirium the dying woman remembered that she had been a princess, and called out, as if addressing an equerry, "To paradise! Quick, quick. Gallop!" Madame Elisabeth, her worthy niece, was prepared for misfortune, for the prison, for martyrdom.

But the last hour had not come; nothing disturbed the shades of Montreuil. French society, on the eve of its great upheaval, was still the plaything of its illusions. As M. Taine has well said, " Everywhere, as this society was approaching its end, there comes a common gentleness, an affectionate softness, like a mild breath of autumn, to soften whatever is hard or dry, and to envelop in a perfume of dying roses the refinement of its moments."

At the Trianon, the Queen, wearing a straw hat, a dress of white muslin, and a gauze neckerchief, watches the milking of the cows, like a farmer's wife. Madame Adelaide takes a violin at a village festival, and, in the absence of the fiddler, plays while the peasant-women dance. The Duchess of Bourbon goes forth in the morning, incognito, to give alms to the poor in their garrets. The King and the Count of Artois help a wagoner to move his mired wagon. Before witnessing the terrible spectacles which the Revolution was preparing, this society, in which the great were becoming intimate with their inferiors, in which it was becoming the fashion to love the country, to return to nature, to delight in the simplicity of rustic manners, to be humane, generous, useful; this society, in which wives followed their husbands to their garrisons, and mothers nurse their children, in which fathers for the first time took an interest in their children's education, — this society, which before the horrible torments of winter, was enjoying the warm autumn sun, was about to see at Montreuil a delightful idyl, an eclogue, with Madame Elisabeth as heroine, which admirably mirrors the tastes of the epoch.

It is a rural story, recalling the country of William Tell, the *ranz des vaches*, the poetic glaciers of Switzerland. Paris and Versailles mingled their tears over this rustic scene, which was like one of Greurze's pictures in its touching simplicity that calls forth both smiles and tears.

At Montreuil Madame Elisabeth led a quiet farm life. The farmyard was full of water-fowl; and her barn was crowded with cows to supply milk to the motherless children of the neighborhood. She was astounded at the number of the children who came after it. Then she enlarged her barn, sent to Switzerland for more cows, and desired to have them put under the charge of a man of that country, an honest peasant on whom she could depend. Madame de Diesbach the wife of a Swiss officer, recommended to her for this position a certain Jacques Bosson, of Bulle, near Freiburg. As he had a father and mother who were very fond of him, Madame Elisabeth sent for them all then. They arrived at Montreuil, and Jacques was put in charge of the barn, which he tended with great zeal. "You must remember," said the Princess, "that the milk of these cows belongs to the children. I shall not take any of it myself until they have all been supplied." Jacques and his parents, when they beheld their benefactress's kindness, exclaimed every moment: "What a kind Princess! In all Switzerland there is nothing more perfect."

Yet Jacques was not happy. There was something lacking; the girl to whom he was engaged was far away, among the mountains; hence his melancholy. One day Madame Elisabeth, who had noticed his sadness, asked the reason. "I thought I had made one person happy," she said to herself, "and I have made two miserable. But the evil can be repaired." Was not the Princess the good angel of her servants as she was of the poor? She sent for Marie, the young girl; she had Jacques marry her, May 26, 1789, and she appointed her milkmaid of Montreuil. Poor Jacques was full of joy.

His melancholy, when separated from his betrothed, inspired a friend of Madame Elisabeth, the Marchioness of Travanet, sister of the Marchioness of Bombelles, with the words and music of a song which court and town used to repeat with effusion:—

> "Poor Jacques, when I was near thee,
>   I did not feel my misery.
> But now, when thou art far away,
>   I know no pleasure in the world;
> When thou camest to share my toil,
>   I found my task light:
> Dost thou remember? Every day was happy.
>   Who will restore to me that time?
> When the sun shines upon our fields,
>   I cannot endure its light;
> When I am in the shadows of the forest,
>   I accuse all nature."

Our grandmothers used to sing us to sleep with his song, the gentle, plaintive charm of which blends with the memory of the kind woman who was Jacques's benefactress.

XV.

CAZOTTE'S PROPHECY.

ALAS! the season for pastorals is nearly at an end. The second part of Madame Elisabeth's life is to present a striking contrast with the first. A sort of religious idyl, of holy eclogue, will conclude this most pathetic drama. The sister of Louis XVI. had a presentiment that too much confidence could not be placed in the virtuous language of the time. She wrote to Madame Marie de Causans, March 24, 1786, this sentence, which was only too accurate: "Although our age is very proud of its tenderness, this is much more a matter of words than of feelings." They imagined themselves living in the Golden Age; it was soon to be the Age of Iron. Suddenly the prospect became dark; the tide rose, the sky clouded, and the air became full of evil omens. The Baroness d'Oberkirch said, in speaking of the year 1788: "There were current at that time in France and in foreign parts many prophecies of different persons. These prophecies found a wide belief; those, especially, of M. Cazotte. A great many people had heard him utter them. But they announced such extraordinary things that reason was compelled to class them with dreams and exaggerations." La Harpe has reported one which was made, he says, by this singular prophet, in the presence of the Duchess of Gramont, early in 1788. Doubtless La Harpe has added to what he remembered, but in the Gramont family as well as in that of the Cazottes, the existence of the prediction is regarded as an authentic tradition.

The Duchess of Gramont had said: "We women are very lucky in having nothing to do with revolutions. It is acknowledged that we, that our sex, shall be spared." "Your sex, Madame," answered Cazotte, "will not protect you this time. . . . You will be treated exactly like men, without the slightest difference. . . . You, Duchess, will be taken to the scaffold — you and a great many other ladies — in the cart, and with your hands behind your backs." "Ah! in that case, I hope I shall have at least a cart draped with black." "No, Madame; greater ladies than you will ride in the cart, and with bound hands, like you." "Greater ladies! What? Princesses of the blood?" "Still greater ladies."

Then, La Harpe adds, the joke seemed to be going too far. Madame de Gramont, to soften matters, passed over this last answer, and merely said in the lightest manner, "You will see that he won't even let me have a confessor." "No, Madame; you will not have one, nor will any one. The last who will be allowed one, will be —"

Then he stopped for a moment.

"Well, who is the happy mortal who shall enjoy this privilege?"

"It's the only one that will be left him, and it will be the King of France."

This strange prophecy was indeed a gloomy one; but however his imagination may have been haunted by gloomy phantoms, can it have foreseen anything to be compared with what actually happened a few years later, May 10, 1794? Let us transport ourselves to that period, and enter the Temple in the evening of May 9.

Ever since she had been separated from the Queen, — that is to say, since August 2, 1793, — Madame Elisabeth had been imprisoned there with her niece, the future Duchess of Angoulême. Their captivity had lasted twenty-one months. Having been kept in close confinement and in absolute ignorance of everything that was going on, — for their sole means of information was the crying of the newsboys outside, — the two prisoners did not know whether Marie Antoinette was living or dead. They confided their sufferings to God; and in their angelic calm and resignation they realized Shakespeare's image of Patience smiling at grief. Every day, Madame Elisabeth used to utter this prayer in company with her niece, to whom she had become a second mother; it was a prayer she had herself composed in prison: —

"What will befall me to-day, O God? I do not know. I only know that nothing will happen which thou hast not foreseen, determined, desired, and ordered from all eternity. That is enough for me. I worship thy eternal and impenetrable designs; I submit to them with all my heart through love for thee. I will everything, I accept everything, I make a sacrifice to you of everything, and I add this sacrifice to that of my blessed Saviour. I beg of thee in his name, and through his infinite merits, patience in my sufferings, and that perfect submission which is due to thee for all that thou desirest or permittest."

The 9th of May, 1794, is drawing to its end; it is seven o'clock in the evening. The two prisoners, who are accustomed to rise very early, are making ready to go to bed, when suddenly they hear their bolts drawn. They hasten to put on the dresses they have just taken off. A man goes up to Madame Elisabeth, and says: "Citoyenne, come down at once; you are wanted." "Does my niece stay here?" "That's none of your business. We shall see about her later." The Princess then embraces her young companion, and says to her, "Be calm; I shall be back soon." A brutal voice calls out, "No; you won't come back! Put on your bonnet, and come down." Madame Elisabeth pressed her niece to her heart: "Well, be courageous and firm, trust always to God; remember the religious principles which your parents gave you, and be faithful to the last counsels of your father and mother." The two captives remained in each other's arms a moment; then the aunt, who is leaving her niece forever, walks away firmly and quickly, with these last words: "Think of God, my child."

She was carried first to the Conciergerie, and then to the Revolutionary tribunal, and after going through the mockery of a trial, she was condemned to death, along with twenty-three other victims. As she was leaving the court-room, Fouquier-Tinville could not keep from exclaiming, "It must be confessed that she has not uttered a word of complaint!" "What should Elisabeth of France complain of?" answered one of the so-called judges. "Haven't we to-day made a suitable aristocratic court for her? There is no reason she should not imagine herself in the Versailles drawing-rooms when she finds herself at the guillotine, in company with all these faithful nobles."

That man did not know what true words he spoke. The execution was to be only an entrance to glory. Madame Elisabeth was to edify, console, and cheer her companions, — Madame de Sénozan, the oldest of the twenty-four victims; the Marchioness of Crussol d'Amboise, formerly the most timid woman in the world, but now most fearless; M. de Loménie, former Minister of War, and Madame de Montmorin, widow of the Minister of Foreign Affairs, who did not lament on her own account, but could not restrain her tears for her son, a young man of twenty, who was also to die. "You love your son," said Madame Elisabeth, "and yet you don't want him to accompany you! You are about to attain all the bliss of heaven, and you want him to linger on this earth where now there is nothing but pain and sorrow." Madame de Montmorin dried her tears, and embracing her son, said, " Come! We will ascend the scaffold together."

The signal is given; the tumbrels start for the Place Louis XV. On the way, Madame Elisabeth continues her exhortations. They reach the place of execution. If it is true, as has been asserted, that Fouquier-Tinville proposed "to bleed those who had been sentenced, in order to weaken the courage they showed in the face of death," he certainly must have had good reason to regret that this measure, which is quite in the spirit of the Revolution, had not been adopted for the batch of May 10, 1794. All the victims, inspired by the presence of the noble sister of the martyred King, showed admirable courage.

The first name called by the executioner was that of Madame de Crussol. She bowed to Madame Elisabeth. "Ah, Madame! if Your Royal Highness would deign to kiss me, I should be perfectly happy." "Very gladly," answered the Princess, "and with all my heart." All the other women enjoyed the same privilege. The men bowed and kissed respectfully the hand of the daughter of kings. One man in the crowd about the guillotine shouted out, " There's no need for all this salaaming; there she is now, like the Austrian!" Madame Elisabeth heard him, and then learned for the first time that she was to meet Marie Antoinette in heaven. One after another the victims ascended the scaffold, and went to the bloody ceremony as the faithful went to the Holy Table. Orders had been given that Madame Elisabeth should be executed the last, in the cruel hope that the twenty-three heads falling before her eyes might perhaps break her courage. It was an unfounded hope. While the sacrifice was going on, she recited the "De Profundis" without a change of color. When the turn of the twenty-third victim, the last but one, came, the saintly Princess said, "Courage! courage and faith in God's mercy." Then it was her time to die, or, rather, to enter into eternal life.

The noble virgin ascended the steps of the scaffold with unfaltering step. She betrayed no emotion, save at the moment when the executioner wanted to take off the neckerchief that covered her breast. "In the name of your mother," said Madame Elisabeth, "do not uncover me." Those were her last words. The soul of Madame Elisabeth was in heaven. All the spectators were moved. Even the knitting women, the Furies of the guillotine, ceased their uproar, and the crowd dispersed in sadness. That day there were around the scaffold none of the usual cries of "Long live the Republic."

Madame Royale, later the Duchess of Angoulême, was left alone in prison, with no more news of her aunt than she had had of her mother. She did not learn their fate till seven months later, when she left the Temple, after an imprisonment of twenty-eight months. Then, when with tears and distress, she was speaking of her relations, a woman, touched by her grief, said, "Alas! Madame has no relatives." "What!" exclaimed the orphan, "Aunt Elisabeth, too! What fault can they have found in her?"

Was it possible that France was destined to behold a repetition of such scenes? Was a time to come when the government, forgetful of the lessons of the past, should lay down its arms, to the terror of good citizens and to the delight of evil ones? The history of the Revolution, which every one thinks he knows, and no one knows sufficiently, cannot be too carefully studied and pondered. It is full of instruction of service to high and low, to rich and poor. What we should seek is not food for wrath, or an inspiration of vengeance, but wise, warning lessons of wisdom and firmness.

When M. Feuillet de Conches published his collection of Madame Elisabeth's letters, he asked a priest to write the preface. We have just read this preface, and we confess that it made a deep impression. The following passage especially struck us: —

"If the whole life of Madame Elisabeth inspires us with a feeling of affectionate reverence and a desire to imitate her virtues, her death, which was a crime as detestable as it was odious, inspires a feeling of horror and indignation for the vile and cowardly assassins who then, under the name of lawmakers, cumbered France with blood and ruin, and crushed it beneath the burden of their vices and their cruelty. I should like to add that it inspires all honorable people with the desire and resolution, not only to declare themselves clearly, but also, if they have any part in public affairs, to act with promptness and energy, so that the vicious shall know what to expect and what caution they must observe. For it is a moving spectacle and one capable of arousing good citizens from their apathy and irresolution, if they would consent to take account of their own force, their rights, and their duties, and not to lose the benefits of their principles by halting counsels and impotent action."

The priest who wrote these lines had no illusions. Something told him that great disgrace, sore trials, immense catastrophes, were impending, and to the page just quoted he added this page which is full of prophecy: —

"Alas! no. . . . Everything begins again on earth, although nothing makes itself over. This is particularly true of revolutions, in which there always is present an imitation of the past which will again be repeated in the future. Although the facts, after the event, show how they might have been prevented or modified, this revelation is denied to the majority; it adopts again the same methods to bring up at the same catastrophes. In the same way, every one knows that there is a certain secret force which carries events beyond the limit fixed by human thoughts and desires, nevertheless, this often-attested truth does not prevent those who collected the clouds from foolishly hoping to control the tempest which they have let loose; it does not render the multitude less confident in the promises of peace and happiness themselves clearly, but also, if they have any part in public affairs, to act with promptness and energy, so that the vicious shall know what to expect and what caution they must observe. For it is a moving spectacle and one capable of arousing good citizens from their apathy and irresolution, if they would consent to take account of their own force, their rights, and their duties, and not to lose the benefits of their principles by halting counsels and impotent action."

The priest who wrote these lines had no illusions. Something told him that great disgrace, sore trials, immense catastrophes, were impending, and to the page just quoted he added this page which is full of prophecy: —

"Alas! no. . . . Everything begins again on earth, although nothing makes itself over. This is particularly true of revolutions, in which there always is present an imitation of the past which will again be repeated in the future. Although the facts, after the event, show how they might have been prevented or modified, this revelation is denied to the majority; it adopts again the same methods to bring up at the same catastrophes. In the same way, every one knows that there is a certain secret force which carries events beyond the limit fixed by human thoughts and desires, nevertheless, this often-attested truth does not prevent those who collected the clouds from foolishly hoping to control the tempest which they have let loose; it does not render the multitude less confident in the promises of peace and happiness with which hypocritical flatterers delude it. The faults continue, and calamities follow close upon their heels."

Who was it that, November 19, 1867, put his name to this preface? It was he who, less than four years afterwards, was to suffer a death as tragic and saintly as that of Madame Elisabeth. It was one of the future victims of the Commune, the Archbishop of Paris, Monsignor Darboy.

XVI.

THE BEGINNING OF THE REVOLUTION.

"DO you know what happened to me the other day?" Marie Antoinette asked Madame Campan some time before the Revolution. "I was going to a special committee in the King's study, and as I was passing through the Œil de Bœuf, one of the musicians said loud enough for me to hear every word, 'A queen who does her duty stays in her own room to look after the roast.' I said to myself, 'Poor man, you are right; but you don't understand my position. I must obey necessity and my evil destiny.'"

And Marie Antoinette sighed, and added, with an accent of profound sadness, "Ah! there is no happiness for me since they have made me out to be disposed to intrigue."

The Queen had a vague instinct of the misfortunes that were threatening her; but she was disturbed and confident in turns, yielding at times to the illusions which the blindest optimism of the epoch evoked in every heart. There was expected some sort of gentle and amusing revolution, a political entertainment, an intellectual tournament, a sort of Fronde perfected by the philosophy and urbanity of the eighteenth century. It was thought that the assemblies would be like meetings of the Academy, the clubs like drawing-rooms, the newspapers like Grimm's *Correspondence*. "The women," to quote from the Duke of Lévis, — for this authority still existed, — "expected to take once more the parts of the Duchesses of Chevreuse and Longueville. The young members of the parliaments counted on their eloquence; the older men, on their reputation; and of the young nobles, some began, in the insignificant meetings of the Freemasons, to practise speaking in public — an art wholly unfamiliar to the nobility in an absolute monarchy. All means were adopted in the hope of winning success."

All were fired by ambition. "Every man who could read," we are told by the Count of Vaublanc, "became a profound politician." From the greatest noblemen down to the idlers in the cafés, every one imagined himself the possessor of an excellent receipt for making good the deficit and saving the country. As M. Aubertin has said, "By all, even by the court party, the Revolution was invoked out of wrath with conflicting ambitions, as well as resentment against the King and his ministers, and the desire of revenge for some vexation or disappointment. The inevitable catastrophe became the last resource even for those on whom it was to fall like a punishment, and in this absurd infatuation of official selfishness, even the courtiers expected from the States-General the destruction of the central power and the restoration of the feudal system."

It was in vain that some solemn souls recalled the tragedies of our history, and the bloody memories of the Ligue. The mournful words of these prophets of evil called forth smiles from this young generation, who, in reply, boasted of the advance of intelligence, the refinement of manners, the progress of science and civilization. These young people laughed at religious fanaticisms, and soon it was to see civil society turned fanatical. But meanwhile any one who pointed out a black cloud on the horizon was regarded as a feeble-minded coward. In this mistaken period, which is called the Golden Age of the Revolution, politics became the fashion, a refinement, a new means of delight for a drawing-room or a boudoir. Titled revolutionaries, in silk or velvet coat, used to discuss the *Social Contract* at some dainty supper. The athletes, before the contest, used to anoint themselves with some prepared essence. There was no discussion, only conversation, and this was full of courtesy and grace. Never had there been more brilliant talk, or more wit and variety; never readier transition from gravity to severity, from wit to seriousness. "What a charm," says the Viscountess of Noailles, " there was in the parties at the beginning of our terrible Revolution, when intelligent and enthusiastic people met in the desire to do good! The old tastes became the refined interpreters of the new ideas. Those of lively imagination hoped soon to see the realization of their wildest dreams; every abuse was gladly denounced, in the hope of rising to a height that should be understood and respected by the masses. In a word, they fell into a well, like the astronomer of the fable, while gazing at the stars." It is in reference to this period of dreams and illusions, of charm and glory, that Talleyrand said when he was old, "No one who did not live before 1789 has any idea of the charm of life."

The great mistake of Louis XVI. was that he let himself be deceived by this mirage; but is it strange that a king was no wiser than his whole generation? His mistakes were those of his time. It would have required a mighty genius to contend with the insubordination which was spreading everywhere. Bachaumont tells us that in 1780 the King congratulated the Marshal of Richelieu on recovering his health. "For, in fact, you are not young; you have seen three centuries." "Not quite, Sire, but three reigns." "Well, and what do you think of them?" "Sire, under Louis XIV. no one dared say anything; under Louis XV. people spoke very low; under Your Majesty they say everything."

The Prince de Ligne has made a very similar remark: "It was as much the fashion, under Louis XVI., to disobey as it had been under Louis XIV., to obey." Disobedience prevailed everywhere, — in the government, in society, in the family, in ideas, and in customs. The nation possibly still loved those who governed it, but it had ceased to fear them. The work of destruction advanced methodically. The leaders of the Revolution had begun by undermining the altar, and that task once accomplished, the throne could prove no firmer.

Doubtless Louis XVI. did not understand the part he should have played. In the place of decision there was uncertainty; in the place of strength, weakness; in the place of single-mindedness, divided counsels, contradictions, vagueness, and the wilful abandonment of all the means of governing. Yet we need not be surprised at the bad advice given to Louis XVI., since, after his bitter experience, we have seen the reappearance of the same corroding theories, — of the same mad theories of political disorganization, and power once more abandoning its proper means of defence.

This is not saying that great reforms were not necessary, urgent, and imperative. Such a thought is far from us; but these reforms should properly have proceeded from a single person, — from the sovereign. There was a social question demanding solution, and this social question should have outweighed the political question. The King might have put himself at the head of this movement, but on the condition of directing it with boldness, and of preserving, at any cost, his regal authority. He should have appeared as the protector, not as the servant, of his people. The details of the edifice — the porches, the pediment, the arcades — might have been modified, but on one condition: that the base — that is to say, the monarchical power — should be preserved. The more important the reforms demanded, the more necessary to strengthen the political and military policy. Instead of remaining at the helm, Louis XVI., when the storm began to growl, called the rashest passengers to take his place.

Why is it that in our own days, Alexander II. succeeded in bringing about peacefully one of the most important of modern reforms; namely, the emancipation of the serf? Because he was able to dispense with calling an assembly. Suppose the Czar had convoked the States-General in order to carry out his programme; in a few months Russia would have been overthrown. Why is the great nation now so powerful? Because its ruler has never listened to this foolish phrase: "A sovereign reigns and does not govern." Reform, instead of rising from below, came down from on high, and hence was accomplished so speedily and so gloriously. All monarchs who wish to bring about reforms ought to be firm in maintaining their own authority. When innovations are not counterbalanced by rigid discipline, they weaken and undermine the power that proposed them.

If Louis XVI. had been a great man, he would, of his royal authority, have proclaimed equality before the law, and, supported by a faithful army, he would have overcome the resistance of the privileged classes with the energy of a Richelieu or of a Peter the Great. The whole people would have followed him in this path, and the strength and glory of the monarchy would only have increased. If Louis XVI. lacked the vigor and determination necessary to push through the reform with an armed hand, if he preferred a silk coat and knee breeches to a uniform, if he abandoned the right of punishing, he ought to have kept close to the old routine, governing in the old-fashioned method of M. de Maurepas, following the advice of his aunts, and above all, making no concessions. The governmental machine, though it seemed worn out, still preserved traces of its former velocity. The States-General would not have convoked themselves. The Count de Vaublanc said with a great deal of justice, "It is not the people who make revolutions; it is the kings and their ministers."

The architect of his own ruin, Louis XVI. proceeded to forge his own chains. The fault lay with the theorists who deluded him, with those men who were forever talking about necessary liberties and forgot indispensable authority; who, when once in power, were compelled to abandon the theories they had held when in opposition. We may truly say, "It is the fate of monarchy in France not to be conquered, but to be betrayed."

The Louis XV. of Madame Du Barry, Louis XV. himself, decried as he was, would never have been guilty of the faults of his unhappy successor. Marie

Theresa, who was thoroughly versed in statescraft, at once saw that the old King's death was a catastrophe. Louis XVI. had a sort of presentiment of his own weakness, when on the day of his coronation he said that the crown tired him. Alas! he shattered his crown and his sceptre with his own hands, and the time came when he was obliged to exchange his diadem for the hideous red cap. A monarch who renounces his prerogatives descends voluntarily from his pedestal. It is like what is called in Roman Law an abdication of civil rights. He who has been master cannot become servant.

XVII.

THE ASSEMBLY OF NOTABLES.

THE more history is studied, the more striking are the illusions which blind rulers. It seems as if Providence put a bandage over their eyes. Louis XVI. had been simple-minded enough to think of crowning the edifice. The Comptroller-General, Calonne, wrote in the paper wherein he proposed convoking the Notables, "The course of time and the changes of events seem to have brought us to the moment in which the monarchy, after long agitation, is at length sufficiently calm and ripe for improving the constitution." The old Marshal of Richelieu asked what punishment Louis XIV. would have inflicted on the minister who should have proposed assembling the Notables. The young Viscount of Ségur said, "The King is handing in his resignation." Marie Antoinette was angry with Calonne, understanding the danger of a parliamentary assembly; but Louis XVI. was so fascinated by his minister's fine phrases that on the day after the council-meeting at which the report had been read, he wrote, "I did not sleep all night, but it was from joy."

Calonne was witty, light, brilliant, fertile in resources, void of malice, ill-will, and rancor, a man devoted to work and pleasure; in short, one of those attractive people who fancy that everything is safe because the victim is adorned with flowers. When he accepted the ministry in 1788, he had promised whatever was asked of him. His entry into favor was a perfect ovation; but soon he had to contend with the incessant demands of the Treasury, and the continual loans produced an unfavorable impression on the public. Calonne failed to see that the deficit was, not the cause, but a pretext of the revolutionary movement which was beginning to assert itself. He lent his aid to a parliament at the very time when a parliament was the most alarming of all the dangers. At first it seemed as if the Notables were going to form a thoroughly conservative assembly. It consisted of one hundred and forty-four members, among whom were seven princes of the blood, fourteen archbishops and bishops, thirty-six dukes and peers. With six or seven exceptions, all the Notables were nobles or enjoyed the privilege of nobility. But it was a political assembly out of the usual order, in a country which had not seen one for a century and a half, and it was, in fact, the germ of the States-General. The Notables assembled at Versailles, February 22, 1787. They held their sessions at the House of the Menus Plaisirs, in the Avenue de Paris, at the corner of the rue Saint Martin, at a place which is now a cavalry-barracks. The main entrance was on the avenue. At the end of the courtyard was a grand staircase leading to a vestibule beyond which was the assembly room; there was another entrance from the rue des Chantiers.

On the day the Assembly of Notables was opened, there was not a single cry of "Long live the King" from the vast crowd watching the procession. As for the cry, "Long live the Queen," it had not been heard for many years. To a sagacious observer it was plain that a great crisis was impending.

Calonne's plan was in itself very good. He wished to establish a proportional equality of burdens, to impose a tax on those who enjoyed privileges, to alienate some of the crown domains, and to extend the stamp-tax. But he lacked the vigor and persistence and the moral weight required for carrying through so bold a programme. Surprise was general when he was heard to pose as a reformer, indeed, almost as a democrat, in his speech; he, the favorite of the Count of Artois, the friend of the Polignacs, the lessor of the courtiers' funds.

"We cannot borrow forever," he said, "nor can we lay taxes forever; we cannot draw upon the future any more; economy will no longer suffice. What, then, is left to us to supply what we need and to procure what is required for the restoration of our financial condition? The abuses. Yes, gentlemen, it is in the abuses that lies a fund of wealth which the state has the right to demand, and which will serve to restore order."

In the same speech Calonne flattered the passions of his time by speaking of the reign of Louis XIV. as "a brilliant reign in which the victories impoverished the state, and intolerance depopulated it." This official utterance of a minister, who thus attacked the memory of a great reign, was a distinct sign of the times. Calonne satisfied neither liberals nor conservatives. Being abandoned by all, he left the ministry six weeks after the meeting of this Assembly of Notables, from which he expected to acquire security; but his plans did not disappear with him, and the Notables adopted the reforms he had proposed. The closing session was held May 25, 1787. The optimists still deceived themselves, and the chancellor, Lamoignon, said in his speech that "everything would be repaired without a shock, without any disturbance of fortune, without modifying the principles of government."

The Archbishop of Toulouse, Loménie de Brienne, succeeded Calonne. The Abbé de Vermont, the Queen's secretary and confidant, had been in former days chosen by the Archbishop to be sent to Vienna by the Duke of Choiseul as tutor of the young Archduchess, who was to become the Queen of France. The Abbé was delighted to see his former protector in the ministry, and regarded the appointment as his own work. "I have more than once heard him say," Madame Campan writes, "that seventeen patient years were not too many for success at court; that it had taken him all that time to accomplish the aim he had set himself; but that at last the Archbishop was where he ought to be for the good of the state." The Abbé became an important person. He had his apartments enlarged in order to have a more appropriate place for the reception of bishops, cardinals, and ministers.

The Queen, who had been a patron of the Archbishop of Toulouse, took more and more interest in political matters. Unfortunately, neither her character nor her education fitted her for this grave occupation. She was ignorant of history, and had read scarcely anything except novels. As the Baron of Besenval said, the moment any one began to talk seriously, her face expressed weariness, and the conversation flagged. Her talk was always desultory, turning from one subject to another. The gossip of the day, stories of the court and the town, gratified her more than discussions about finance. She was ill at ease in the political circles in which she was destined to live, and she herself regretted that she was called upon to rule. She had insensibly acquired complete ascendancy over her husband. "Whether through superiority, or fear, or charm," the Baron of Besenval says elsewhere, "not only did he never oppose her, but I have seen more than a thousand times that when she was speaking, his eyes and mien expressed a feeling, an eagerness, which the most dearly loved mistress seldom evokes."

Marie Antoinette had the best intentions in the world, but she lacked the persistence and decision necessary for one who is to rule. She made a mistake in calling Brienne to the charge of affairs. This philosophic prelate, whose wit was more admirable than his morality, and whose learning was superior to his judgment, had been recommended by the general opinion — a fact which somewhat excuses the Queen. As Madame de Staël said: "His ecclesiastical dignity, combined with his constant desire to attain the ministry, had given him the external appearance of a statesman, and his reputation encouraged this impression, until he was given an opportunity to belie it. . . . He admired in turn the conduct of Cardinal Richelieu and the principles of the Encyclopædists; he tried acts of force, but he drew back at the first obstacle. . . . Arbitrary and constitutional in turn, he was awkward in both systems, which he tried alternatively. . . . Defeated as a despot, he allied himself with his old friends, the philosophers, and, out of humor with the privileged classes, he tried to please the nation." In a word, he personified the principle of the pendulum, which, everywhere and at all times, is the method of weak governments.

He made one blunder after another. Everybody expected a royal session, in which the King should have the Parliament record in one mass all the edicts adopted by the Notables. Instead of that, Brienne was ill-advised enough to send in the edicts one after another. Parliament defended the privileges, and yet remained popular by being in opposition. The

Palais de Justice became a seat of revolution; the stairways and courtyards were crowded with a hired multitude, with no opinions of their own, belonging to no party, but united by the attraction of a salary, and turbulent or calm, according to the orders it had received. If a resolution seemed violent, the warmer were hand-clappings and bravos and cheers with which these gentlemen were rewarded as they left the meeting.

The Parliament played a sad comedy, and was rapidly approaching the hour of its suicide when it sustained abuses while putting on a mask of liberalism. When the imposition of a stamp-duty came up for discussion, July 6, 1787, it demanded, as the Notables had done, information on the financial status. When the ministry refused to accede to their request, one of the councillors, the Abbé Sabatier, called out, "We demand the status; it's the States-General we want." This play on words was very successful, and soon turned into a formal proposition. The Parliament expressed a desire to see " the nation assembled before any new impost was laid." The members of the legal corporation composed songs about the Queen, calling her Madame Deficit, and the anger against her grew so violent that, by advice of the lieutenant of police, Louis XVI. forbade her to show herself in Paris.

The Baron of Besenval gives the following account of a conversation he had at this time with Marie Antoinette in the garden of the Trianon: "I told the

Queen that it was in vain that she flattered herself on winning over the Parliament; that the more she temporized, the more its boldness would increase; that it was time for the King to show that he meant to be master, and to have his own way by acts of authority; otherwise he would have to lay aside the crown, and possibly forever. 'Ah!' the Queen exclaimed, 'M. de Calonne has done a great deal of harm to the country with the Notables!'"

Still everything might have been saved. With the exception of the cities with parliaments, the whole kingdom was perfectly quiet. The populace still kept its religious and monarchical sentiments. Discipline prevailed in the army. With a little vigor Louis XVI. might have preserved his rights. Instead of that, he had recourse to half-way measures. After having exiled the Parliament to Troyes, August 15, 1787, he had the weakness to call it back. He let the Duke of Orleans organize the Revolution. With inconceivable blindness, he permitted the publication of a mass of anarchic pamphlets and libels. Nothing else was read. Booksellers exposed these incendiary writings before the eyes of the public. They were read aloud in public places, under the very eyes of the police. Soldiers were forbidden to use their weapons in case of disorder in the street. This blundering order encouraged evil-doers, and soon they attacked the watch and burned the guard-houses.

When the Parliament returned from Troyes, in

September, 1787, the younger lawyers and their hirelings illuminated the neighborhood of the Palais de Justice, and broke the windows of those houses whose owners were courageous enough to withstand the demand of a troop of rioters. Calonne was burned in effigy in the Place Dauphin. Manikins representing Breteuil, the Minister, and the Duchess of Polignac, the friend of the Queen, were carried through the crowd, amid imprecations and abuse. A little more, and the image of Marie Antoinette would have been treated in the same way. "From a chaos of tranquillity," wrote Mirabeau, "France has passed to one of excitement." The Parliament, protesting against the King's bed of justice, November 19, 1787, said in its list of grievances: "Such measures are not in accordance with your heart; such examples are not Your Majesty's principles; they spring from another source." These mutinous words were an allusion to the Queen. Brienne, though he governed so badly, clung eagerly to power. He exchanged his bishopric of Toulouse for that of Sens, which was much more lucrative, thus acquiring a revenue of six hundred and seventy-eight thousand francs; and moreover had himself presented with a timber privilege, to the value of nine hundred thousand francs, to pay his debts.

Everything became disorganized. The exile of the Duke of Orleans to Villers-Cotterets, the arrest of the Councillor d'Espremesnil, the limitation of the powers of the parliaments, the formation of a full court for the registration of edicts, failed to check the ever-growing spirit of revolt. Serious trouble broke out in many parts of the kingdom. The King, gliding rapidly down the fatal path of concession, decided to convoke the States-General, which the insurgents so noisily demanded. A resolution of the Council, August 8, 1787, appointed May 1, 1789, for the holding of the States-General, which were so fatal to the monarchy. It was the date set in the preceding year by the prophetic spirit of Mirabeau, the future tribune. The old régime itself determined the hour of its own death.

A few days later (August 25, 1788), Brienne, succumbing beneath the weight of his unpopularity, left the ministry; and Louis XVI., conquered by new ideas, called to power the friend of the liberals, the great banker, the celebrated theorist, the author of the famous *Report*, the idol of the philosophers and of the admirers of the English constitution, the father of Madame de Staël, — Necker, the Genevese. There was a moment of enthusiasm; for a few hours the Queen enjoyed a breath of popularity; but the opposition to her only redoubled in intensity when it became known that Brienne, who had been supposed to be in disgrace, was going to receive a cardinal's hat. Events brought out the character of this prelate, one of the four who gave their adhesion to the civil constitution of the clergy. Put into disgrace by a brief of Pius VI., declaring him deprived of all ecclesiastical dignities, he boasted of having been one of the promoters of the Revolution, and presented himself as a candidate at the election to the legislative assembly, as constitutional bishop of Sens, and in spite of all his concessions, nothing but his sudden death saved him from the guillotine. Marie Antoinette cruelly repented the protection she had given him. "I have seen the Queen," Madame Campan wrote, " shedding bitter tears over her wrongs at this period, when Brienne, shortly before his death, dared to say in a speech which was printed, that a part of what he did during his ministry had no other object than the healthy crisis which the Revolution had brought about."

Necker was an honest man and a skilful financier. He was a slave of public opinion and very desirous of popularity; and thus, like all such people, was carried further than he had intended. Although a fervent Royalist, he prepared the Republic without knowing it. The Revolution began in the early days of his second ministry. The Parliament was exceeded, like Necker himself. He declared that the States-General should be convoked regularly, according to the form observed in 1614; that is to say, according to conservative rules. Nothing more was needed to deprive the old assembly of the popular favor in a single day. Its army of advocates, attorneys, notaries, practitioners, students, deserted it. The Parliament was already punished for its opposition to royalty, and its attacks against the crown turned against itself. Its end was not a natural one; it died by its own hands.

Necker called the Notables together again, to lay before them questions relative to the composition and form of the States-General. They met for the second time at Versailles, November 6, 1788. Was the Third Estate to have a representation equal to that of the nobility and clergy? Were the votes to be taken by classes or individually? The whole Revolution lay in the way in which these two questions were settled. An enormous majority of the Notables pronounced against the double representation of the Third Estate, and yet Louis XVI. was imprudent enough to place himself on the side of the minority. This was the opinion of Marie Antoinette, who, despite her fears, still had illusions. In vain did the Count of Artois, the three Condés, and the Prince of Conti address a memorial to the King, in which they denounced "the Revolution which was preparing in the principles of government." The unhappy monarch, misled by his exaggerated kindness, was fascinated by

> "that spirit of independence and error,
> The forerunner of the fatal fall of kings."

The Queen was persuaded that the *bourgeoisie*, represented by the Third Estate, was devoted to the throne, that the lower clergy would be held by the hope of preferment; that Necker would have authority over the lawyers and others of that class who composed the Third Estate. The Count of Artois, who held the contrary opinion, almost quarrelled with

Marie Antoinette. The Duchess of Polignac and all her society sided with the Prince against the Queen. Distraught by so many intrigues and such contradictory counsels, the unhappy Queen could find no peace in her friend's drawing-room. She still went there, in order not to betray any change in her habits, but she was greeted with such cold respect that she always went away in sore distress.

December 27, 1788, Louis XVI., "in accordance with the wishes of a minority of the Notables, the demand of the provincial assemblies, the opinion of publicists, and the many addresses presented on this subject," ordered that "the number of the deputies to the States-General should be at least one thousand, and that the number of the deputies of the Third Estate should be equal to that of the clergy and nobility together." When the news of this royal declaration became known, Paris illuminated. The monarchy was lost.

XVIII.

THE PROCESSION OF MAY 4, 1789.

FORTY years before 1789, one of the Ministers of Foreign Affairs of Louis XV., the Marquis d'Argenson, wrote these prophetic words: "There prevails a philosophic wind of free and anti-monarchical government. Possibly the revolution will meet with less opposition than is expected; it may take place by acclamation. . . . All classes are discontented at the same time; a riot may easily grow into a revolt, and a revolt into a revolution, in which there would be elected tribunes of the people, comitia, communes. . . . The whole nation would take fire; and if it became necessary to assemble the States-General, these states would not assemble in vain. It will be well to take care."

It must be said in justice to Marie Antoinette that she understood that the summoning of the States-General would be fatal to royalty. On the day when she learned that Louis XVI. had decided to convoke them, she happened to be coming from the public dinner; she detested all the splendor, which was at once painful to her eyes, and sought refuge in her bedroom, where she stood in the embrasure of the first window, gazing into the park. She sent for Madame Campan, and said to her: "Heavens, what is this news we hear to-day? The King has permitted the States-General to be summoned." Then, raising her eyes to heaven, she added, "I am very much afraid that this important event is a gloomy token for France." And her eyes, filled with tears, were turned to the ground.

Marie Antoinette perceived that she was betrayed on every side. The clergy, far from trying to appear as a mediator, sought only to encourage the opposition, and blindly followed a few restless, stubborn, and vain bishops. The nobles, a feeble, inharmonious body, made annoying murmur, as the Baron of Besenval expressed it. The Anglomania of which the young men and the women were the victims turned them from an interest in horse-races to a passion for politics. Even in the King's ante-chamber the most seditious utterances were heard.

The men who should have been the Queen's most chivalrous defenders, such as the Duke of Orleans, the Duke of Lauzun, the Marquis of La Fayette, had become her foes. She, with her loyalty, kindness, and generosity, was amazed at human ingratitude, and nothing could explain to her the violent and unjust hatred which pursued her. Even the ministers, instead of supporting the throne, only weakened it. Augeard tells us in his interesting Memoirs, that the Queen said to him in May, 1789, "Do you think that M. Necker wishes to deceive us?" "I don't know, Madame, that M. Necker wishes to deceive us, but I am sure that he deceives himself. For the state, it is exactly the same thing." "What! M. Necker would make us stake our kingdom double or quits?" "Madame, I should deem you lucky in that case; Your Majesties would have one chance in your favor; now I don't know a single one." "Heavens, what do you say?" and the Queen burst into tears.

Marie Antoinette was of the opinion that the States-General should meet at some town distant sixty leagues from Paris, instead of being convoked at Versailles. Necker successfully opposed this wise opinion. The councillors of Louis XVI. had reached the highest pitch of blindness and imprudence. As the Count of Vaublanc said: "The ministers were ignorant of the history of France, or they would have known that before Louis XVI. no king had conceded any part of his own authority. . . . They would have remembered that when Anne of Austria, in her regency, desired to convoke the States-General, the great Condé, whom she consulted, told her that a prince of the blood ought to lose his life before enduring the convocation of these states which had wrought so much harm to France."

The summoning of the States-General was, alone, a great fault; but what rendered this fault irremediable was the choice of Versailles as the place of meeting. "How," to quote from the Duke of Lévis, "how could boldness have been carried so far as to establish an assembly to control the destinies of France, and one in which so much preponderance had been given to the popular party, at a distance of four leagues from the capital, which was a centre of intrigue and corruption, and crowded with a populace excitable and open to bribery."

The lot was thrown. These States-General which had been so long awaited, which were regarded as an instrument of salvation, as a universal panacea, were about to meet. The first session was appointed for May 5, 1789.

A great religious ceremony opened in peace the era of tempests. There was a solemn procession which took place the evening before the day the Assembly was to be opened, to pray for the blessings of God upon their work. The throne and the altar, before being overthrown, arrayed themselves in majestic pomp, and the ancient monarchy, which was doomed to perish by one concession after another, appeared once more with the prestige and ceremony of its venerable glory.

This flame, which was so near extinction, was scattering its final rays, lighting the horizon like a setting sun, and the same people who were about to utter cries of fury and vile blasphemies against their God and their King, still sang canticles, and walked piously in a procession. On that day Robespierre himself carried a candle.

There is now in the palace of Versailles a hall called the Hall of the States-General, and is so called from the pictures it contains, representing these assemblies. Especially noteworthy is a long and fine frieze painted by M. Louis Boulanger: the subject is the procession of May 4.

At ten in the morning, Louis XVI., clad in the royal robes, and accompanied by the princes of his family, all wearing the robes of the different orders, issued from his apartment. He entered a state carriage with the Count of Provence and the Count of Artois. At the coach doors were the young Dukes of Berry and Angoulême and the Duke of Bourbon. The Queen was in another carriage. The princesses and the princes of the blood came next. This magnificent procession was to go to the church of Notre Dame. After a short prayer, the procession began to form, headed by the banners of the two parishes: that of Notre Dame in front, next that of Saint Louis. Then came the Recollects, followed by the parish clergy. After them marched the deputies of the Third Estate, in two parallel lines, each one, like all in the procession, carrying a candle. They were dressed in black, with a little silk cloak, a cravat of white muslin, a three-cornered hat without edging or buttons. After the Third Estate came the nobility. The deputies wore a very rich dress, — a black cloak with a gold facing, a lace cravat, white silk stockings, and a hat with white feathers, turned up like that in which Henri IV. is always represented. Then followed the deputies of the clergy, in two files, separated by the royal musicians, the body-guard and the Swiss soldiers. In front were the deputies of the town clergy; behind them, near the canopy under which was the Holy Sacrament, marched cardinals, archbishops, and bishops. The canopy was carried by the high officers and gentlemen of honor of the King's two brothers. The front strings were held by the Dukes of Angoulême and of Berry; the hind ones, by the Counts of Provence and of Artois. Under the canopy, the Archbishop of Paris carried the Holy Sacrament. The King was among the high officers of the crown, in the middle of the two files following the canopy. The Queen was at the head of the left-hand file, in which were the princesses and their ladies. The right-hand file was composed of princes of the blood, dukes, and peers. At the head marched the Duke of Chartres (later Louis Philippe). He was followed by the Prince of Condé, the Duke of Bourbon, the Duke of Enghien, the Prince of Conti. Then came the dukes and peers. The French and Swiss guards were drawn up in line from the church of Notre Dame, where the procession started, to the church of Saint Louis, whither it proceeded. The way was strewn with flowers, rich stuffs, and the crown tapestries decorated the streets. The crowd was enormous. A magnificent spring sun lit up this festival of church and crown. Those of the princes who were too young to take part in the procession were allowed to look at it. The Dauphin was in the great stables; the Duke of Normandy (Louis XVII.) and Madame Royale (the Duchess of Angoulême) were at the windows of a house in the rue de la Paroisse Saint Louis, opposite the pavilion Beauregard. Starting from the church of Notre Dame, through the rue Dauphine, the Place d'Armes, the rue Satory, the rue de l'Orangerie, the rue de la Paroisse Saint Louis, — that is the route of the procession.

The sight of the Holy Sacrament, the religious pomp, the pious songs, the odor of the flowers and of the incense, the cheering sunlight, gave hope for a brief moment to the heart of Marie Antoinette, who warmly prayed God for a good result to France. Suddenly, ominous clamors aroused the gloomiest presentiments. The Queen, as she passed, heard some women of the people, those who later, doubtless, used to knit at the foot of the guillotine, crying out, "Long live the Duke of Orleans!" with such evident ill-feeling that she turned pale and nearly fainted. She was supported by some of her suite, who feared for a moment that it would be necessary to stop the procession. But the courageous sovereign, for whom the future had so many trials in reserve, soon recovered herself. The procession reached the church of Saint Louis, where mass was said. Like the Divine Master, whose sacrifice was commemorated, the pious Louis XVI. was to have his Calvary. On his return to the palace he was greeted by an enthusiastic crowd. Hosannahs still sounded; but soon the "Let him be crucified" was to be heard.

XIX.

THE OPENING SESSION OF THE STATES-GENERAL.

MAY 5th opened the most famous assembly of modern times, — one which put an end to the old régime and began a new world. From early morning Versailles was in a turmoil; everywhere it was felt that a solemn event was about to begin.

Let us take a look at the assembly-room before the arrival of the deputies. The place is that in which the Notables used to sit, — the Hôtel des Menus Plaisirs, near the palace, in the Avenue de Paris, at the corner of the rue Saint Martin. The room is twenty feet broad and fifty-seven long, and is surrounded with fluted Ionic columns without pedestals. In the ceiling there is an oval opening, and the light which comes through this passes through a screen of white silk. In the aisles benches have been arranged for the spectators, and at a certain height there are bays with balustrades. At the end of the hall rises a platform for the King and the court; it is semicircular, and is elevated a few feet, and covered with a carpet of violet velvet with gold fleurs de lis; above it is a grand canopy, with its rim fastened to the columns.

The throne stands under a magnificent baldaquin decorated with long golden fringes. To the left are a large armchair for the Queen, and stools for the princesses; to the right were camp-stools for the princes; at the foot of the throne, to the left, was an armchair for the Keeper of the Seals; to the right, a camp-stool for the High Chamberlain; at the foot of the platform, a bench and a large table for the Secretaries of State; on each side of this table are benches reserved for the fifteen Councillors of State and the twenty Masters of Requests invited to the meeting, as well as for the Governors and Lieutenants-General of the provinces. Running lengthwise in the hall are other benches — those on the right, for the deputies of the clergy; those on the left, for the deputies of the nobility; at the end, opposite the throne, for the deputies of the Third Estate. The floor is covered with handsome carpets from the Savonnerie factory.

The meeting was to open at one o'clock in the afternoon. At nine in the morning every gallery, every bench, was occupied. Two thousand persons were in their places. With the exception of the tribune set apart for the diplomatic body, all the front benches were reserved for ladies, who all wore their finest dresses.

Between nine and ten the Marquis of Dreux-Brézé and two masters of ceremonies began to arrange the deputies in their places according to their bailiwicks. This took two hours. Necker's appearance was greeted with a round of applause. Two other rounds broke forth when the Duke of Orleans was seen entering with the deputies of Crépy-en-Valois, and insisting that the *curé* of the deputation should enter before him. The nobles wore a black cloak with gold stuff, and a cocked hat *à la Henri IV.* Their splendor presented a marked contrast with the modest and colorless dress which etiquette demanded to be worn by the deputies of the Third Estate, who appeared, with a sort of defiant humility, in black coats, short cloaks, and hats without bands or buttons. The cardinals wore their red caps; the archbishops and bishops, in the front row of the benches destined for the clergy, appeared in rochets, camails, square caps, and violet cassocks. The deputies numbered in all 1183: of these 291 were clergy; 270, nobles; and 622, of the Third Estate. The King-at-Arms and the four heralds, dressed in armor, were stationed at the entrance of the hall. Sentinels, under arms, stood in each tribune, and in every place between the columns.

When all had found their place, the King and Queen were notified, and they at once made their entrance, accompanied by their suite. The moment the King appeared, the whole assembly arose and broke into enthusiastic applause; cries of "Long live the King!" burst forth on all sides. This tumultuous uproar was followed by a long and respectful silence so long as Louis XVI. remained standing while the court took their places. General admiration was felt for the calmness of this good and generous monarch's expression, for the confidence it wore, and for his majestic and paternal air. The Queen seemed less easy; but her somewhat pensive and anxious face was lit up by a few smiles before the warm greeting of the three orders.

Louis XVI. wore his royal robes, and a hat with feathers and ribbons, adorned with diamonds. He raised his hat for a moment, put it on again, and then read with much dignity a speech which reflected all the noble feelings that animated his heart. Everything which could be hoped for from the tenderest interest for the public happiness, everything which could be demanded of a sovereign, the first friend of his people, could be expected of their King by the deputies of the three orders. This speech, which was read with perfect ease and a lofty air, was frequently interrupted by applause. At that moment Louis XVI., in the consciousness of his honesty and of his loyal and pure intentions, doubtless imagined that France was capable of understanding him.

After the King, the Keeper of the Seals spoke, recalling all the sacrifices His Majesty had made, and was still ready to make, to establish the general happiness on the basis of public liberty. Then it was Necker's turn. The reading of his report took three hours; it was listened to with the deepest attention.

There is now to be seen at Versailles a fine picture, painted by M. Auguste Conder, which represents the session we have just described. The moment selected by the artist is that in which Necker is standing before the ministerial bench, delivering his speech. In front, to the left, are to be seen, among the deputies of the clergy, Saint-Aulaire, Bishop of Poictiers; Lefranc de Pompignan, Archbishop of Vienne; Boisgelin, Archbishop of Aix; and Talleyrand, Bishop of Autun. To the right, in front of the Third Estate, sits Boissenot, deputy from Bordeaux; in the next row, Bailly; in the third, the Breton workingman Gérard, deputy from Rennes; in the fourth, Barnave and Robespierre; in the fifth, Chappelier; further still, Mirabeau, and near him, the Abbé Sieyès; and finally, on the last bench, to the extreme right, Rabaud de Saint-Etienne, Kauffmann, and Duport. At the end is the place for the deputies of the nobility, where are to be distinguished the Duke of Rochechouart, the Marquis of La Fayette, Casalés, the Duke of Richelieu, the Duke of Liancourt. In front of the three orders is Louis XVI., seated on his throne; on his left are Marie Antoinette, Madame Elisabeth, Madame Adelaide, Madame Victoire; on his right, the Count of Provence (Louis XVIII.), the Count of Artois (Charles X.), the Duke of Berry, the Duke of Angoulême, the Duke of Chartres (Louis Philippe).

When the ceremony was over, the King rose and remained standing for a few minutes. Then His Majesty departed amid the applause of the whole assembly, and cries of "Long live the Queen!" mingled with cries of "Long live the King!"

Optimists imagined that everything was saved;

wiser heads thought all was lost. Madame de Staël, who was in the gallery with Madame de Montmorin, the wife of the Minister of Foreign Affairs, expressed her delight and her hopes for the country. "You have no reason to feel happy," answered the Minister's wife; "from all this there will issue great disasters to France and to ourselves." Madame de Montmorin was right: her husband was slain at l'Abbaye in 1792; she herself and her son were guillotined.

At last the States-General, who opposed to the King what they called the Nation, were invested with terrible powers. The real nation was with the King, whom it loved and honored, whose loyalty, kindness, and virtue it esteemed and admired. But there were a few ambitious spirits who, in the hope of imposing upon public opinion, were determined to try to have it believed that a handful of revolutionaries was the French people. The unhappy monarch fell blindly into the snare which his enemies had laid for him. Marie Antoinette, charming, affable, and amiable, flattered herself perhaps that she would be able, by the charm of persuasion, to bring back to kindlier feelings those who had strayed away; but this, alas! was an error. Nothing can correct or improve men of bad faith. The Queen soon perceived the singular malevolence to the royal family and the court which the deputies had brought from their provinces. She heard, with amazement, their strange questions about the King's alleged intemperance and the Asiatic luxury of the Trianon. Since the simplicity of this country-seat, which was far less sumptuous than many bankers' houses, did not correspond with the idea which certain deputies had formed of it, they maintained, when visiting the Little Trianon, which was the subject of a number of stupid fables, that the most extravagantly furnished rooms were closed to them. They insisted on being shown an imaginary drawing-room, which they said was decorated with diamonds, and with twisted columns covered with rubies and sapphires. The Queen of France was compelled to be civil to these uneducated and malicious men. She did the honors of Versailles with exquisite grace, and with untiring kindness, talked with them about their families and their local interests. There were some deputies who puritanically refused to go to court. They were soon to be Republicans, if they were not already. They lodged at Versailles, in the houses of revolutionary citizens, who, from stupidity or jealousy, retailed the most ridiculous stories, the vilest calumnies about the Queen. Other deputies, to be sure, expressed to her devotion and respect, but a secret instinct told her that whatever she might do, she was a marked victim of fate. At times she would have a gleam of hope, and her natural energy would inspire her with confidence in her power to brave every peril and avert every stroke of fate. Soon, however, she fell back into her customary anxiety, and she felt crushed, overwhelmed, by a hand of iron. She saw in the future a bottomless pit, a gulf of fire and blood, to which all concessions were swiftly bearing her. Something told her that while to-day resistance was possible, to-morrow it would be too late. But everything stood in her way, — her husband's weakness, the ministers' sophistries, the blindness and selfishness of all who surrounded her, the revolutionary passions which were breaking out in even the highest ranks of French society. What could she hope for in that situation? What can a woman, however generous and brave she may be, do against a combined world?

XX.

THE DEATH OF THE DAUPHIN.

EVER since the opening of the States-General, Marie Antoinette had been anxious and restless. Since she could scarcely sleep, she used to go to bed very late and meditate on the ever-serious incidents of the day. One evening, towards the end of May, the unhappy Queen was sitting in her bedroom, talking with Madame Campan about the morning session. There were four candles burning on the dressing-table. One went out of itself; Madame Campan lit it again. Then the second, and soon the third also, went out. Then Marie Antoinette, clasping in alarm the hand of her faithful companion, exclaimed : "Misfortune makes me superstitious. If the fourth candle goes out like the other three, nothing can prevent my regarding it as an evil omen ! " — the fourth candle went out.

At that very moment a terrible blow was hanging over the Queen's head : she was about to lose her oldest son, the young Dauphin, whose birth, seven years before, had filled all France with joy and congratulations. For many months he had been ailing. While apparently in flourishing health he was suddenly attacked by the rickets which curved his spine, hollowed his face, and made his legs so weak that he had to be helped in walking, like an infirm old man. His suffering and exhaustion were omens of another death-struggle, — that of the monarchy.

Already in the previous year, Marie Antoinette knew the catastrophe which threatened her as queen and as a mother. When, at the formal reception of the ambassadors of Tippoo Sahib in 1788, she appeared on her grand throne, in the Hall of Hercules, majestic, resplendent, covered with the richest of the court jewels, and the representatives of the Asiatic monarch, dazzled by the more than Oriental luxury, ecstatically admired, more than the statues and pictures; more than the silver and gold, than the embroideries and diamonds sparkling everywhere, the beauty of the unrivalled Queen, — this proud woman before whom every one was prostrating himself as before an idol, hid beneath her diadem the cruelest anxieties.

From this reception of the Asiatic ambassadors, one child was absent, — the Dauphin. The young Prince had been very anxious to be present, but he was already so reduced that his appearance would have made a painful impression on the company, and Marie Antoinette was unwilling to have him appear. And so at the very moment when it was probably thought, amid all this pomp and show, that the Queen of France and Navarre was enjoying to the full the happiness of power and pride, her heart was torn by keen anguish. She knew that the heir of this mighty throne was condemned, and beneath her crown this poor mother and hapless queen felt iron nails that pierced her brow. Does it not seem as if every one who entered the palace of Versailles was cursed by fate? The Indian ambassadors were put to death by their master, and in a year this imposing French court was broken up. These great lords and ladies were forced to emigrate, or if they stayed they paid the penalty with their lives. Grass was to grow on the pavement of the palace, and the former sanctuary of the absolute monarchy was to become a vast sepulchre. What sadder story can be found than that of the Dauphin's fate, whose baptism was celebrated January 21, and who died at the very moment when there opened an assembly, fatal to the monarchy, and whose sufferings were a sort of prelude to those of his brother, the martyred child, who was to bear the title of Louis XVII.?

Since April 16, 1789, the young invalid had been quartered at Meudon, but neither the wholesome air of this place nor the tender care which encompassed him could prolong his life. A few hours before his death, he asked M. de Bousset, his valet de chambre, for a pair of scissors; he then cut off a lock of his hair, and wrapped it up carefully in a piece of paper. "See here, Monsieur," he said to his valet de chambre, whom he dearly loved, "this is the only present I can make to you, for I own nothing else: but when I am dead, you will give that to papa and mamma; when they remember me, I hope they will remember you."

The child died at the age of seven years and seven months, in the night of June 4, 1789, one month to a day after the opening of the States-General. He drew his last breath in the arms of his mother, to whom he was heard to say that he only suffered at seeing her cry. This cruel loss broke the Queen's heart, and her sufferings turned her hair white, though she was but thirty-four years old. She had her portrait painted about this time; and when she gave it to Madame de Lamballe, she wrote underneath, "Unhappiness has turned her hair white."

June 5, the body of the Dauphin was exposed in the castle of Meudon, on a state-bed. The 8th, the princes of the blood and deputations of the three orders went to sprinkle holy water in the coffin. The 13th, the heir to the French crown was buried in the Abbey of Saint Denis very quietly, in the presence of but a few persons.

Poor boy! He was lowered, as Bossuet says, to that subterraneous dwelling, "to sleep in the dust with the great of the earth, with the vanished kings and princes among whom there is hardly room for him, so close are the ranks, so quick is death to fill the gaps." Alas! the quiet of his grave was not to be defended by the guard of kings, his ancestors, who had preceded him to the grave. To desecrate a child's tomb and to scatter his ashes is an exploit befitting the heroism of Jacobins. And what day do they choose for this odious task? October 16, 1793, the day when his unhappy mother, who had so mourned her boy, was led to her execution. Yes, at the very hour when Marie Antoinette bowed her head on the scaffold, the exhumers of kings hastened to Saint Denis to tear the great of the earth from their tombs, to melt the lead of their coffins, and to throw into a common ditch their despoiled bodies. In this sacrilegious work they grew jealous of death, and like vultures disputed their prey; and that day they profaned among other graves those of Henrietta of England, of the Princess Palatine, of the Regent, of Louis XV. Compare the two scenes, — the scaffold of Marie Antoinette and this desecration of the tombs at Saint Denis, — with the transport of joy that, twelve years before, had hailed this child's birth and greeted his mother's happiness; then ask in what romance, however gloomy and terrible, you can find anything more moving and more terrible than the contrast between such realities.

XXI.

THE ADVANCE OF THE REVOLUTION.

THE end of governments is seldom a natural one; it is generally a suicide. They generally perish because, while they possess the force of right, they hesitate to use the right of force. A sort of madness leads them to lay down their arms, to spike their guns, to dismantle their fortresses, and to surrender, bound hand and foot, to their irreconcilable enemies. Those sovereigns who sacrifice their indispensable authority to necessary liberties are like the lion in love: they let their talons be clipped and their teeth be drawn. Then they blame others for faults which in fact are but the result of their indecision and weakness. They weaken themselves, forgetting that the first duty of a government is self-defence; that an unpunished riot is a dishonor, a slap in the face of the prince who endures it; that the control of order should outweigh all other considerations, and that it is a cruel thing to let many thousand innocent victims perish to spare a few criminals. There are circumstances in which a ruler has no right to withhold punishment; when pity is only weakness and humanity simply abdication. No monarch who hesitates in face of a revolt deserves to rule. What would one think of a soldier who should fear to use his weapon on the battle-field? Politics is a battle.

An honest man, whose Memoirs, Guizot has said, will be much read, though less than they deserve, — Malouet, the last politician, according to Burke's expression, to watch at the bedside of the expiring monarchy, — says, with justice, that there is no excuse for the ministers of Louis XVI. "That King," he says, "had a just mind, which would have made him adopt the wise combinations proposed to him, if, instead of showing him the difficulties and dangers of firmness, they had convinced him of their necessity."

And how could the ministers reduce him, at the end of 1788, to a real suspension of his royal functions through the indecision with which they let him approach the question of the States-General? It was no longer the King who spoke, but the consulting attorney of the crown, asking counsel of everybody, with an air of saying to every man he met: "What must I do? What can I do? What part of my authority is it desired to retrench? What will be left to me?"

M. Charles Aubertin justly says in his excellent book, *L'Esprit public au dix-huitième siècle*, that it took Louis XVI., with all his faults, three years to bring about a dethronement which was mainly his own work, and that he took all this time to descend from a throne from which now one falls in a few hours. At the beginning of the Revolution all Frenchmen, even Marat and Robespierre, were Royalists, and, as Michelet has remarked with truth, the one of the three orders most favorable to royalty was the Third Estate. Mirabeau announced his intention to attack the bureaucratic despotism in order to exalt the royal authority. The situation was in no way desperate.

It is the fashion nowadays, in a certain historical school, to represent accomplished facts as the consequence of an inevitable fatality, which prudence, wisdom, and genius would have been powerless to resist. To us nothing seems more opposed, not merely to the freedom of the will and to human dignity, but also to the philosophy and majesty of history, than this Mohammedan fatalism which deprives the affairs of this world of their interest and moral value. In our opinion M. Aubertin is right in saying, "How frivolous to believe that events which have never been resisted, that unrestrained and unscrupulous passions, would have followed the same course if a firm will had undertaken to direct and control them!" We agree with M. de Montlosier in thinking that, with such aid as was afforded by the conduct of Louis XVI., the upheaval might have taken place in even the richest and most prosperous kingdom in the world. The Count of Vaublanc completes the accuracy of this remark by an axiom which is thoroughly confirmed by the history of the nineteenth century:

"In France it is always the ruler and his ministers who overthrow the government."

Malouet accurately judged the faults of the martyred King when he said: "Between the King and his council there was an alternation of mistakes about everything which might be regarded as a prudent or a vigorous measure. Thus the King, who had a passive courage, felt a certain shame about leaving Versailles; he was perfectly conscious of the danger, but he hoped to avoid it by a display of strength. When it was necessary to use it, he could not decide to draw his sword on his subjects. I linger with regret on this unhappy monarch's faults; for, with his kind heart, he deserved a different fate: there was a certain captain of the grenadiers who would have saved him if he would have let him."

Louis would have been puzzled if he had been asked exactly what it was he wanted. He wavered between the nobility and the Third Estate, between the old régime and the new. All his actions and all his words were full of humanity, kindness, and justice. He was a philanthropist, an honest and a virtuous man, but he was not a king. The prey of the illusions of a period given up to vain dreams, he could not believe in evil, and he judged others by himself.

As for Marie Antoinette, who was justly alarmed by her husband's indecision, her position was most painful. It was not easy for her to urge vigorous measures, and an appeal to force when her husband was all weakness. As a worthy daughter of Maria Theresa, she naturally inclined to energetic decisions. She would have liked to ride before her troops; but this was impossible when Louis XVI. opposed every demonstration of force, and was absolutely unwilling to abandon the paternal attitude which suited the wishes of his heart and his instinctive tendencies.

Meanwhile the peril was increasing from day to day. June 17, 1789, the Third Estate, with some members of the clergy, announced itself to be the National Assembly. June 20, the deputies found the hall in which they met closed by superior order, and they went to the Tennis Court, and took the famous oath.

June 23, Louis XVI. published an order establishing the maintenance of the three orders, and commanding the deputies to separate. At the same time he decreed *motu proprio* the greatest reforms, — the abolition of the pecuniary privileges of the nobility and the clergy, commercial liberty, the establishment of provincial states, and a number of innovations, each more liberal than the others. In his speech he uttered this sentence which is full of noble optimism: "I can frankly say that never has a king done so much for any nation; but what other has so well deserved it by its loyalty as the French nation?" And he closed his harangue with these words: "If you desert me in this noble undertaking, I shall alone establish the welfare of my people. It is possibly a rare occurrence for the monarch's sole ambition to be that his subjects shall agree to accept his benefits."

Six months earlier this declaration would have met the idea and the desire of the States-General; but it came too late, especially when the government had not decided to put an end to the Assembly. This indecision of those in power encouraged the Revolution, and Mirabeau was able to utter to the Grand Master of Ceremonies the famous phrase, which would have been impossible a few weeks before: "Go tell your master that we are here by the power of the people, and that we shall be driven away only by the force of bayonets."

To save the crown and France Louis XVI. had four things to do, — to acknowledge of his own will, by virtue of his sovereign power, what are called the principles of 1789; to dissolve the States-General; to exile the Duke of Orleans; to have the rioters shot. If he had done these things, Louis XVI. would have been a great man; but he preferred to be a victim. There is no need of speaking about fatality; the only fatality was the King's weakness. He was the author of his own fall.

June 23, the unhappy monarch must have seen the gulf toward which all his concessions were driving him. Necker, who was always desirous of popularity, had refused to accompany Louis XVI. to the royal meeting, which, in the eyes of Marie Antoinette, was an act of treachery or of cowardice. Well, at the very moment when the nobles imagined that everything was righted by the sort of bed of justice which the King had just held, and when the Queen, holding her son in her arms and displaying him to her faithful servants, indulged in a blind confidence, outcries were heard in the palace courtyard. It was the crowd calling Necker, and noisily congratulating him on not having taken part in the royal meeting; then they carried him home in triumph, and made him appear at his window amid frantic applause. The Queen herself entreated Necker not to resign his portfolio. The true King of France was no longer Louis XVI.: it was the Genevese banker.

In Paris, disorder grew steadily. The populace, allured by bribery, prepared for the approaching insurrection. At the Palais Royal, which had become a hotbed of anarchy, the most incendiary motions followed one another without interruption.

June 30, rioters broke open the prison of the Abbaye, and set free several of the French guard who were confined for insubordination. At last Louis XVI. seemed to awake from his torpor. In accordance with the advice of the Queen, and of the majority of the ministers, six thousand men were cantoned in the Champ de Mars. Twelve thousand men were encamped at Versailles and in the suburbs of Paris. The Marshal of Broglie was put in command of the troops. He established his headquarters in the palace of Versailles, and turned the garden into a camp. His ante-chamber was crowded with orderlies and officers ready for service. He had put a regiment in the Orange House. The royal party was divided into a group of optimists and a group of alarmists; while these last thought everything lost, the others spoke with scorn of the masses of the populace, saying that "one need only pull down his hat over his eyes to disperse them, and that when the time had come, one did not know how to pull down his hat." Louis XVI. did not know to which side to listen. His brothers counselled vigorous action; Necker dissuaded him from it. Every regiment that arrived gave the Genevese minister more annoyance. As the Baron of Besenval reports, "Every argument which was brought up to him fell to the ground before the possible anger of the National Assembly."

There was a lack of harmony between the Marshal of Broglie, in command at Versailles, and his subordinate, the Baron of Besenval, in command of Paris. A fatal blunder had been made in leaving in garrison in the capital the regiment of French guards who had been corrupted by the revolutionary propaganda. Confusion was wide-spread. The troops, perceiving that they were insufficiently led, and the police, perceiving that they were not properly supported, became demoralized. It was not a camp of six thousand men that should have been established in Paris, but one of sixty thousand. No preparations were made to defend the Bastille, and there was not a single regiment to protect the arsenal of the Hôtel des Invalides. The ministers of Louis XVI., as weak in strategy as in politics, were incompetent to take the most rudimentary precautionary measures.

July 11, the King perceived, a little late, the errors into which Necker had led him. He urged that minister to leave without telling any one of his departure. Necker obeyed, and at once betook himself to Switzerland, not even informing his daughter. The Marshal of Broglie entered the new ministry. But the military measures were so incomplete and clumsy, the number of the troops was so small, the dread of shedding the blood of the rioters had so paralyzed the government, such scandalous impunity had been accorded to the revolutionary doings of the Palais Royal, every arm of power had been so weakened, that the catastrophe broke forth.

Malouet says very truly: "The Reign of Terror, which was not proclaimed by the pure Republicans till 1793, will be acknowledged by every impartial man to have begun in 1789. The first club of the Palais Royal (the club of Valois, of which Sieyès, then a partisan of the Duke of Orleans, was one of the founders), and then the Breton Club, which became the Jacobin Club, were the inventors of this infernal machine, which might easily have been destroyed before it exploded." But what could be expected of a government that let the troops be attacked with insulting language, stones, and pistol-shots, "while the soldiers made no threatening gestures in reply, so great was their respect for the order not to shed a single drop of citizens' blood"? The capture of the Bastille, so vaunted by the Revolution, was no difficult feat. That famous fortress was garrisoned by only a hundred soldiers, almost all disabled, and there was not a single regiment to defend its approaches.

The insurrection had begun July 12. The troops who had assembled that day in the Place Louis XV. were thoroughly discouraged when they saw that their commanders would not let them use their weapons. Neither the police nor the army could save a government against its will. The 13th, the gun-sellers' shops were pillaged, and the Paris militia was organized, which was to become the National Guard. The morning of the 14th, the rioters had taken all the arms from the Hôtel des Invalides, which was entirely without means of defence. "The disorder grew from hour to hour," says the Baron of Besenval, "and my embarrassment also increased. What plan was to be followed? If I should let my troops get engaged in Paris, I should start civil war. . . . Versailles neglected me in this cruel situation. . . . I decided that the wisest course was to withdraw the troops and leave Paris to itself." The 14th, there were three Swiss regiments still encamped in the Champ de Mars, with eight hundred mounted men, hussars, and dragoons. The prevailing opinion of the general officers who were assembled at the Military School was that nothing of importance could be accomplished by so small a force. While at the other end of Paris the rioters were taking possession of the

Bastille, the troops did not stir. That evening they withdrew to Sèvres, in accordance with the orders of the Marshal of Broglie.

What was going on at Versailles while the army was thus retreating before the Revolution? The previous evening the Assembly had begun a session which was to last sixty consecutive hours amid confusion and alarm. It was rumored that the King was preparing to flee; that the Queen, the Duchess of Polignac, and the princes had been seen in the Orange House, distributing food to the officers and men; that in the night of the 14th, Paris was to be attacked at seven points, the Palais Royal surrounded, and the National Assembly dissolved. News came of the attack upon the Bastille, and every one listened to hear the distant roar of the cannon. The Assembly, in terror, sent to the King one deputation after another. To the first Louis XVI. made reply that he had just ordered the withdrawal of the troops from the Champ de Mars, and that having been informed of the formation of the Civic Guard, he had appointed officers to command it. To the second he said: "Gentlemen, you wring my heart more and more by what you tell me concerning the unhappy events in Paris. It is impossible that the orders given to my troops should be the cause." The Bastille had been captured, July 14, at half-past five in the evening, and Louis XVI. had gone to bed before any one had consented to break the fatal news to him. It was his faithful officer, the Duke of Liancourt, Grand-Master of the Wardrobe, who, in spite of the ministers, woke him up and told him what had happened. "What a revolt!" exclaimed the King. "Sire," replied the Duke, "say rather, what a revolution!"

XXII.

THE DEPARTURE OF THE DUCHESS OF POLIGNAC.

THE Bastille had just been taken. The insurgents who had conquered without a struggle, imagined that the next day they would be confronted by an imposing force, and did not dare to show themselves. Versailles intimidated Paris, and Paris intimidated Versailles. There were still many regiments on whose fidelity Louis XVI. could absolutely count. Nothing would have been easier for him than to withdraw to a fortified city at some distance from the capital, and there to speak like a king. But it was in vain that Marie Antoinette counselled energetic measures; he preferred dismissing the troops and playing a sentimental part before the Assembly. He appeared there on the morning of the 15th, with no escort or guards, accompanied only by his two brothers.

Standing bareheaded, with no sign of pomp, without even using the armchair placed on the platform, the heir of Louis XV. seemed to be begging forgiveness of the subjects who had defied his authority. "You were afraid," he said; "well, it is I who have confidence in you." His speech was simple and touching. The deputies applauded the amiable monarch, and accompanied him on foot to the palace. The courtyards were filled with a vast throng. They asked the King, Queen, and their children to appear on the balcony. Marie Antoinette asked Madame Campan to fetch the Dauphin. The Duchess of Polignac, the governess of the royal children, understood that she was not to accompany the young Prince, and she exclaimed, "Oh, Madame Campan, what a blow I have received!" Then she kissed the Dauphin and withdrew to her own room, in tears.

After taking the child to the Queen, Madame Campan went down into the courtyard. Threatening words were spoken there with sullen wrath. "I know you very well," muttered one veiled woman. "Tell our Queen not to meddle with the government. Let her leave her husband and the good States-General to make the happiness of the people." "Yes, yes!" exclaimed a man dressed like a produce porter, "tell her that these States are not like the others, which were of no use; that the country is too intelligent not to get some good from them; and that there will not be a single deputy of the Third Estate to speak with one knee on the ground. Tell her that — do you understand?"

At that moment the Queen appeared on the balcony above the marble courtyard. "Ah!" said the veiled woman, "the Duchess of Polignac isn't with her." "No," added the man, "but she's still at Versailles. She's like a mole, and works under ground; but we shall know how to get a spade to dig her out."

In the afternoon, as Madame Campan was passing along the terrace on her way to Madame Victoire, she saw three men arrested under the windows of the throne-room. One of them shouted loudly, "That's where the throne is, and soon people will be hunting for pieces of it." Then all broke out into abuse of the King and Queen. One of these was Saint-Huruge, one of the men of the Duke of Orleans.

Meanwhile, deputations of fishwomen kept coming to ask Louis XVI. to return to Paris, and the agitation continued in the rebellious city. What was he to do? Obey the demands of the populace and plunge into that seething abyss, or withdraw from Versailles with the faithful troops whom he had just ordered to retreat? Marie Antoinette, whose instinct did not deceive her, urged the second course. She had already burned a number of her papers and put her most valuable jewels in a strong box which she meant to take with her. But in the morning of the 16th, it was decided that the troops should depart without the King, and that the unhappy monarch, trusting to the loyalty of his good city of Paris, would go alone, the next day, to his rebellious subjects.

From the moment that Louis XVI. adopted this resolution, it became impossible for the Count of Artois, the Princes of Condé, and the Polignac family to stay longer in France. The King ordered them to leave. In vain the Count of Artois, who was courage personified, offered to enter the insurgent city alone, or at any rate to accompany him on his visit appointed for the morrow; Louis XVI. declined the generous offer, and bade the Prince to leave the kingdom at once, together with his two sons, the Dukes of Angoulême and of Berry. The same order was given to the Prince of Condé, to his son, the Duke of Bourbon, to his grandson, the Duke of Enghien, and to the Prince of Conti. The three sons of France and the four princes of the blood obeyed, with despair in their heart, and in the evening of July 16 took leave of the King, whom they were never to see again.

At almost the same moment, at eight o'clock in the evening, the Queen sent for the Duke and Duchess of Polignac. With a voice broken with emotion, Marie Antoinette stammered out: "The King is going to Paris to-morrow; if he is asked — I fear the worst. In the name of our friendship, leave. . . . There is yet time to save you from the fury of my enemies; by attacking you they mean to attack me. Do not be victims of your devotion and of my friendship."

It was necessary to leave at once, without delay — in a few hours, at midnight. This departure seemed to them desertion, and dishonorable. Their devotion and courage could not consent to such a sacrifice. At this moment the King entered: "Come," the

Queen said to him, "help me persuade these honest people, these faithful officials, that they must leave us." Louis XVI. approached sorrowfully the Duke and Duchess. "My cruel fate," he said to them, "compels me to send away all whom I esteem and love. I have just bidden the Count of Artois to leave; I give you the same order. Pity me, but do not lose a moment; take your family with you; count upon me at any time. I shall keep your offices for you." And as he spoke the King burst into tears. Marie Antoinette kissed the Duchess, and the two friends parted forever.

In less than three hours the preparations for departure were finished. This Duchess, who was thought very rich, and whom the libellous writers of the time represented as one of the principal causes of the deficit, went away poor from Versailles, where she had been so calumniated, and at the last moment the Queen was obliged to give her a purse of five hundred louis to pay her travelling expenses. M. Campan put her in her carriage at midnight. She was dressed like a chambermaid, and took her seat in front. With her were her husband, her daughter, the Duchess of Guise, her sister-in-law, the Countess Diane, and the Abbé de Balivière. Just as she was starting she received this note from Marie Antoinette: "Good by, dearest of friends! What a painful word it is, but it is necessary! Good by! I have only strength enough to kiss you."

Sad fate and destiny! This beautiful and charming Duchess, whose success had aroused much jealousy, friend of the Queen, governess of the royal children, was now treated like a condemned criminal. A moment before she had been told that the hour of exile had come, and that she could not see the sun rise at Versailles. She could not be allowed to give one last glance at the beautiful park, at its familiar shades; but she must depart at once, at midnight, in disguise: it is all like a hideous nightmare. And then imagine the distress and anxiety that pursued the fugitives in their journey! Was the Queen they had left to be saved or lost? and the King, who was to start for Paris in the morning, would he be alive in the evening? That throne, with no army to defend it, would it be overthrown? When would end this exile, begun so gloomily?

On their way they heard threats and imprecations. If the fanatics who were declaiming against the authorities had known that the passing carriage contained the detested Polignacs, they might fear the worst. When they got to Sens they found that the populace had risen. An inquisitive crowd came up and asked them: "Do you come from Paris? Are the Polignacs still with the Queen?" The Abbé de Balivière remained perfectly calm, and answered quietly: "The Polignacs? They are now a good way from Versailles. Those evil persons have been got rid of."

At the next stopping-place a postilion got up on the step, and said to the Duchess: "Madame, there are some faithful people in the world; I recognized you all at Sens." And the Duchess slipped some louis into his hand.

While the Polignacs were hurrying towards Switzerland, Louis XVI., with a courage that equalled his honesty, was facing the populace of Paris alone, carrying words of peace and union. It was with the liveliest apprehensions that Marie Antoinette saw him depart. She feared that he might be detained as a hostage, or, possibly, be put to death. Nevertheless, he set forth in the morning of July 17. Twelve men of the body-guard and of the civic guard of Versailles accompanied him as far as the Point du Jour, near Sèvres, when they left him, and their place was taken by the new National Guard of Paris. In their ranks were some of the French guards, who had taken part in the insurrection at the capture of the Bastille on the 14th. For artillery they had the cannons taken from the Bastille and the Invalides, and these trophies of rebellion seemed to threaten the King's carriage. One musket went off, and mortally wounded a woman. People asked one another with alarm what would become of Louis XVI.

It was after four in the afternoon that the King, who had left Versailles at ten in the morning, reached the Hôtel de Ville in Paris. Encompassed by a throng full of sullen hostility, the amiable monarch, to whom Bailly had just said, "Henri IV. had conquered his people, to-day it is the people who have reconquered their King," mounted the steps of the staircase, beneath an archway of crossed swords, which were as much a menace as an honor. The attitude of the crowd continued cold. Not a cry of "Long live the King!" had been uttered. Louis XVI. appeared on the balcony; Bailly gave him the tricolored cockade, and he fastened it on his hat. Then the crowd applauded; the usual cheers rent the air. The good father, who fancied that he had recovered the love of his children, wept for joy. "Cubières," he said to one of his equerries, "the French loved Henri IV., and what King ever better deserved their love?" Ah! it was not of Henri IV. that Louis XVI. should have been thinking, but of Charles I.

Meanwhile Marie Antoinette, in a fever of anxiety, was counting the minutes. At one moment she was pacing up and down her room, at the next she was on her knees, praying God to be merciful. Every hour messengers brought her the news from Paris. She had already heard how coldly Louis XVI. had been greeted at his entrance. Convinced that her husband would be held as a hostage, she exclaimed, "They will not let him come back!" She blamed herself for not going with him. If he became a captive, she determined to share his fate, and to surrender herself, with her children, to the National Assembly, making them a speech which she already knew by heart. It began thus: "Gentlemen, I come to place in your hands the wife and the family of your King; do not suffer earth to separate those whom Heaven has joined." She sent for several of her courtiers, but their doors were found locked; they had fled in terror. A death-like silence prevailed in the palace. The little Dauphin stood with his face pressed against the window-pane, looking anxiously up the Avenue de Paris, eagerly awaiting his father's return. "Why," he asked, "why should they hurt papa? he is so good."

At last, at about ten o'clock, carriage wheels were heard. It was the King, coming back safe and sound, pleased with the day and contented with his people. Marie Antoinette uttered a cry of joy, and ran to meet her husband. On the steps of the marble staircase they fell into each other's arms. Versailles was full of rejoicing; the crowd, carrying branches of trees, in token of its delight, made its way into the palace courtyard. The King appeared twice, with his family, on the balcony, in answer to the cheers and applause. He kept repeating, as he recounted the events of the day: "Happily, not a drop of blood was shed. I swear that not a drop of French blood shall ever be shed by my orders."

In short, the courage, the generosity, the kindness of the King had been admirable; but something more was needed to direct the masses. If they were not held in awe by force, their hearts softened but for a moment, to resume speedily their violent passions. Louis XVI. deceived himself when he thought that he had tamed the savage monster by his gentle looks; the next day it was to roar again.

XXIII.

THE QUEEN AND THE MARQUIS OF LA FAYETTE.

THE moment was approaching when Marie Antoinette was to find herself in conflict with two men who had been her courtiers, whom she had made her debtors by her kindness, and whom the vicissitudes of politics were going to make her enemies. One was the Marquis of La Fayette; the other, the Duke of Orleans. No one, a few years earlier, when the monarchy was at the height of its glory, would have imagined that a marquis and a prince of the blood would suddenly become the idols of the revolutionists, and would hold in check the heir to the throne of Louis XIV. Periods of disturbances, are, however, fertile in just such surprises, and the leading actors must themselves often be surprised at the part which fortune leads them to play in the drama of history, which is full of unexpected turns and changes.

Early in the reign of Louis XVI. we saw the young Marquis of La Fayette in the charming court of Marie Antoinette. He was one of the young men who tried to revive the dress of Henri IV., and who, in the quadrilles at the Queen's balls, wore silk doublets and caps with white feathers. He was born in 1757, and his father and mother having soon died, he came into possession of a vast fortune. In 1774, when sixteen years old, he married a girl of fourteen and a half, Adrienne de Noailles, daughter of the Duke of Ayen, who was himself the son of the Marshal of Noailles, and of Anne Louise Henriette d'Aguesseau. The Marquis of La Fayette lived with his wife and her parents in the rue Saint Honoré, in the splendid Noailles mansion, which stood where now runs the rue d'Alger. At that time he had a cold and serious air, which seemed to indicate shyness and timidity, and presented a marked contrast to the sprightliness, frivolity, and witty talkativeness of his friends. Beneath this cloak of apparent coldness was hidden an ardent nature, the mainspring of which was an unbounded love of fame. He had been devoted to women before he became ambitious of glory. The Count of Ségur could not keep from smiling when the Marshal of Noailles said to him, "Do use your influence with La Fayette to warm his coldness, to arouse him from his indolence, to give him some of the fire of your character." "Better than any one," explains the Count, "was I able to understand him, for in the previous winter (1776) he had been in love with a very beautiful and charming woman, and had taken it into his head that I was his rival; hence, although we were friends, in an access of jealousy, he had spent nearly a whole night with me, trying to persuade me to contend, sword in hand, for the heart of a beauty in whom I took not the slightest interest."

Great was the surprise in Paris and at Versailles when it was learned that this nineteen-year-old sage, who seemed so cold and indifferent, had, against the King's orders, chartered a ship at his own expense, and crossed the ocean to fight for American liberty. Without a regret he left the delightful court life, his magnificent home, the meeting-place of elegance and intelligence, to plunge into the wildest adventures. His wife, who was devoted to him, showed Christian stoicism, and did not try to detain him. In 1807, shortly before her death, her husband recalled this distant memory. "Do you remember the first time I went to America? At M. de Ségur's wedding you concealed your tears. You didn't wish to seem distressed, lest it should make people think ill of me." "True," she said, "it was very thoughtful for a young girl. But how kind it is of you to remember it all this while!"[1]

Although La Fayette had committed an act of disobedience by going to fight under the American flag, Marie Antoinette never forbore to treat him with great kindness. She often received him when he returned to France in February, 1779, and with her own hand copied these lines from the tragedy of "Gaston and Bayard," in which the Marquis's friends thought they saw a resemblance to him: —

---

[1] *Life of Madame de La Fayette*, by Madame de Lasteyrie, her daughter.

"Profound in his plans, which he forms with coldness,
It is for their accomplishment that he preserves his ardor.
He knows how to defend a camp and to storm walls;

He loves battle like a young soldier;
Like an old general he knows how to avoid it.
I like to follow him, and even to imitate him.
I admire his prudence and love his courage;
With these two virtues a warrior is never old."

La Fayette was the fashion. The famous battle of Beaugé, in which an ancestor of his had defeated and killed the brother of Henry V. of England, and saved the crown of Charles VII. of France, was not made more of than was the battle of the Brandywine, in which the descendant of the illustrious warrior was wounded in heading a charge of the American troops. When he returned to America for the second time, the government could not praise him too much or find benefits enough wherewith to reward the young champion of the new republic.

January 21, 1782, a great festival was taking place at the Hôtel de Ville in Paris, in honor of the birth of the Dauphin, when suddenly word came that La Fayette had just reached the capital. Madame de La Fayette, who was at the Hôtel de Ville, then received an unusual mark of the Queen's favor and bounty; for Marie Antoinette herself carried her in the royal carriage, to the Hôtel de Versailles that she might as soon as possible welcome her husband. Every one became enthusiastic over the conqueror of Cornwallis; the infatuation was universal. At his suggestion the Queen had her full-length portrait painted, and she sent it to Washington. The King promoted him over all his fellow-officers, to raise him to the rank he had held in America. His bust was placed in the Hôtel de Ville in Paris. His wife happened to be at an audience of the upper house of Parliament the same day as the Grand Duke Paul, and the Attorney-General of the Court of Peers complimented her, as well as the son of the Empress Catherine.

This reforming Marquis, who on his return to his native land, could show the scars of the wounds he had received in fighting for freedom, a republican decoration (that of the Cincinnati), to whom the United States had given the rights of citizenship, and Washington had treated like a son, came back more American than French, full of zeal for an exotic liberty which, when transplanted in France, was to bear fruits very unlike those he expected. In Paris he had a board set up in a handsome frame; there were two columns: on one was inscribed the American Declaration of Independence; the other was left blank as if to await a similar Declaration on the part of the French. Intoxicated with popularity, he delighted in what he called "the delicious sensation of the smile of the multitude." He said himself that his reputation was a portion of his happiness without which he could not live; his perfect confidence in his own ideas, his unfailing hopefulness, his canine love of fame, as Jefferson called it, his resolution to disregard all the lessons of experience, his firm faith in a golden age, even in one of iron, composed a character which was a curious mixture of heroism and simplicity. The Duke of Choiseul has named him Gilles Cæsar; Mirabeau used to call him Gilles the Great.

"To judge him," M. Thureau Dangin has said, "it is only necessary to remember that he was always the man of the National Guard. He was in some way the incarnation of this grand illusion of civic liberalism. Having been called to the head of the National Guard, in 1789, after the fourteenth of July, he was given the same place in 1830. He called it his eldest daughter, and under the Restoration used to sign his manifests, "A National Guard of 1789."

With all his obstinacy and fixity of purpose, he had a momentary hesitation before entering the path he so boldly followed. This was on the 22d of July, 1789. He had just been appointed commander-in-chief of the new militia, the National Guard, which flaunted the tricolor cockade, and had enlisted in the French Guards, who were devoted to the Revolution, a certain number of Swiss, and many soldiers who had deserted their regiments in the hope of better pay. With this revolutionary militia he expected to be able to maintain order — an illusion which he soon lost. July 22d he saw an old man, one Foulon, seventy-six years of age, murdered before his eyes, in spite of every effort on his part to save the poor victim, who had been dragged to the Hôtel de Ville with nettles around his neck, a bunch of thistles in his hand, a truss of hay behind his back, and was then hanged on a lamp-post by veritable cannibals. The Reign of Terror was beginning. On that day the Marquis of La Fayette was indignant; he handed in his resignation, but, allured by the flattery of the populace, he hastened to withdraw it. Mirabeau said at the time, " Nations require victims," and Barnave, " Was the blood that was shed so pure ? "

After this brief flash of clear-sightedness, La Fayette fell back into his customary illusions. Although Louis XVI. and Marie Antoinette had honored him with such great kindness, and his birth should have attached him to the monarchy, he who in less troubled times would have been one of the noblest and most faithful of the King's servants, was about to be led by a fatal chain of events to weaken the throne which it was his first duty to defend. The spirit of opposition was most prominent in this great democratic nobleman, a revolutionist and a conservative by turns, who one day fomented a riot, and the next day repressed it; who seemed to Louis XVI. and the Queen now like an enemy, and in a moment like a friend.

Moreover, in 1789, he was no longer able to control events. In the morning of October 5, the Parisian rabble, which had gathered in front of the Hôtel de Ville, was shouting, " To Versailles ! to Versailles ! " La Fayette opposed this proposition. He rode up and down in front of a battalion of the National Guard which was drawn up on the quai de Grive, trying to gain time, in the hope that the crowd would abandon its plan. A young man who belonged to the battalion stepped out of the ranks, seized the bridle of his horse, and said, " General, hitherto you have commanded us; now we are going to lead you." La Fayette looked at this young man, and in compliance uttered but one word, "March!"

XXIV.

MARIE ANTOINETTE AND THE DUKE OF ORLEANS.

THE Duke of Orleans, who was to be one of the most dangerous of the enemies of Marie Antoinette, was for a long time on good terms with her. The correspondence of the Count of Mercy-Argenteau shows no sign of any serious dissension between the Queen and the Prince. During the visit to the court of the Archduke Maximilian, in 1785, there were some few trifling matters of etiquette about which the Prince complained; but that was all. The Prince, who was then styled the Duke of Chartres, becoming Duke of Orleans only in 1785, at the death of his father, was born at Saint Cloud, in 1747. At the beginning of the reign of Louis XVI. he was a young man of twenty-seven, devoted to pleasure and utterly indifferent to politics. The Queen treated him very kindly, and he took part in all the entertainments which she gave. In 1769 he had married the daughter of the Duke of Penthièvre, and by this alliance he had come into possession of an enormous fortune, which the untimely death of his brother, the Prince of Lamballe, had made still greater, permitting him to live most extravagantly.

In 1776, the Princess of Lamballe was able, by her influence with the Queen, to secure for the Duke the post of governor of Poitou. The same year, with the Count of Artois, the companion of his pleasures, he established horse-races, which was a favorite amusement of Marie Antoinette. January 30, 1777, he gave the Queen a grand ball at the Palais Royal. The next day this paragraph appeared in the *Journal de Paris:* " To-day, at midnight, His Highness the Duke of Chartres gave a ball at the Palais Royal, to which the Queen and the royal family were invited." This statement was not perfectly correct: a queen is never invited to an entertainment; she honors it with her presence. But in spite of what was said about it, the Queen willingly overlooked the blunder.

In 1777, the Duke of Chartres served with distinction on the ocean and in the Mediterranean. Having been appointed admiral, he was present in 1778, at the battle of Ouessant, in the *Saint Esprit*. It was by misunderstanding the signals, and not through lack of courage, that he sailed out of action, at the decisive moment, with the ships under his command. For a time the public reproached him with this blunder, and it has been asserted that Marie Antoinette blamed him in the most cutting way; but the Count of Mercy's correspondence does not corroborate this statement. On the contrary, the ambassador represents the Queen as treating the Duke at this time with the warmest interest. November 17, 1778, he wrote to the Empress Maria Theresa as follows: —

"The Duke of Chartres, who has been blamed for the loss of the victory at Ouessant, and has been, in consequence, in hot water with the high naval officers, appealed to the Count of Artois, who persuaded the Queen to give to the Duke of Chartres the benefit of her protection. It had been suggested that he should honorably resign from the navy, and receive in return some special mark of distinction. For this purpose it had been proposed to revive the post of colonel-general of hussars and light cavalry; but the King opposed those plans, and it required all the Queen's influence to carry them through. She gave them all possible aid."

No one at that time could have suspected the future that awaited the Prince. The traditions of his family were rich in examples of fidelity to the monarchy. Without mentioning the brother of Louis XIV., who was all obedience and submission, his great-grandfather, the Regent, had exhibited the utmost devotion to the young Louis XV.; his grandfather, whose last years were spent at the Abbey of Saint Geneviève, lived and died like a saint; his father, whose second marriage was a morganatic one with Madame de Montesson, was an amiable and kindly man, who took no interest in politics, and never in any way embarrassed Louis XV. or Louis XVI. With such models, the Prince, who later was to be called Philippe Egalité, did not seem destined to play a revolutionary part.

Led by circumstances, he had no idea whither he was going, and when he started he had no thought of the abyss to which he was marching. The bare thought that he might become a regicide would have brought a smile to his lips. He was a witty, pleasant-tempered man, more eager for pleasure than for glory; always in love, and especially with Madame de Buffon, like a youth of eighteen; averse to work, careless, extravagant, with no settled plan of life; devoted to the pleasures of the table, to hunting, luxury, the theatre, races, gambling, and English fashions; capable of shining in boudoirs more than in public life; distrustful of the demagogues, whom, however, he was always following; more truly a courtier than a friend of liberty; rather weak than wicked; more to be pitied than blamed; a sad and noteworthy example of what the revolutionary spirit can make out of a sympathetic nature.

One of his most faithful friends, the beautiful Madame Elliott, an Englishwoman, thus speaks of him: "The Duke of Orleans was a very amiable man, with great charm of manner, of a yielding disposition: never did there exist a man less fit to be the head of a great party. His mind, his talents, his education, in no way adapted him to this position; and for a long time I hoped that his heart would revolt at the thought of bringing his country to such a cruel condition of anarchy. His revolutionary friends at last understood him, for they could not induce him to take any interest in their plans. Some of them were lucky enough to patch up a peace with the court, leaving the poor Duke in the hands of the wretches who surrounded him, and introduced to him others of the same kind, until at last they had brought him to ruin and disgrace."

Madame Elliott, who was as kind as she was intelligent, continues with an emotion which was easily understood: "All this is painful for me to say; for I had known the Duke of Orleans many years, and he had always been very kind and attentive to me, as he was, for that matter, to all who had anything to do with him. No one can form any idea of the way I suffered when I saw him gradually sinking into every sort of infamy, for I am thoroughly convinced that he never meant to go so far."

At first the Duke's opposition was very gentle. He made frequent visits to England, and brought back the English fashions, ways, and amusements, as well as their political ideas. He was very enthusiastic about parliamentary institutions, and persuaded himself that France ought to become a mixed monarchy, in which the first prince of the blood should be the leader of the opposition. But opposition is a complicated bit of machinery into which one cannot thrust his finger, without getting his arm, and finally his whole body, caught. The downward path is easy and fatal; it begins in the drawing-room, and ends in the street. At first one excuses one's self by calling patriotism and love of the public welfare what is really rancor or ambition. A man deems himself a good citizen, when he is, in fact, an insurgent.

It is easy to set limits which are never to be passed,

but soon they are found too narrow. Things get more confused; calmness and moderation are lost. A man hates his enemies less for the harm they have done him than for the harm he has done them. A sincere reconciliation soon becomes impossible; an attempt is made to patch one up, but on both sides there survive defiance and hatred, and the kiss of peace is a Judas kiss. Unhappy are those families in which the head has to treat and argue with those who owe obedience! Officers should command respect from their soldiers; professors, from their pupils; masters, from their servants; fathers, from their children; sovereigns, from their subjects, and especially from the princes of their household. The higher a man's place in the monarchy, the more incumbent it is upon him to set an example of submission to the sovereign; and kings have no excuse for not enforcing this rule upon princes of the blood who are disposed to neglect it. Both the Duke of Orleans and Louis XVI. were guilty: one, of rebellion; the other, of weakness. Instead of commanding and acting like a master, the good-natured monarch remained, in spite of his cousin, in one of those equivocal situations which give a king the advantage neither of severity nor of kindness.

Rendered bold by the impunity he enjoyed, the Duke himself was surprised at the freedom that was given him; at the incompetence and indifference of the police; at the ease with which the Palais Royal, which a few good patrols could have speedily mastered, became the headquarters of revolt. The Prince soon learned to despise a government which was so weak, so feeble, so undecided. A king who put himself under guardianship, who resigned one by one all the prerogatives of authority, inspired him with nothing but contempt. The Duke imagined himself justified in anything. The needy intriguers, who desired to get what they could out of him, inspired him with ambitious ideas which he had not known at first, and these led him to his ruin. Possibly he was vain enough to imagine that he alone could govern France, and tried to justify his conduct to himself on this pretext.

Marie Antoinette did not deceive herself about him. She knew that the Duke of Orleans was henceforth an enemy with whom reconciliation was impossible. But, we repeat, the fault lay with Louis XVI., whose duty it was to crush the opposition at the beginning. Instead of that, the King tried half-way measures. If he did exile the Prince, the exile was only a short excursion. He let the Duke organize resistance while the Notables were sitting. At the opening of the States-General, he allowed him to sit among the deputies, for the sake of popularity, instead of on the platform, which was a proper place for a prince of the blood. He permitted the Palais Royal to become the seat of a second monarchy, a Parisian monarchy, full of revolutionary feeling, with its budget, its officials, its army; he suffered Paris to be flooded with papers and pamphlets preaching anarchy — that the revolt should have its troops enrolled and paid. Never has a government so surrendered its powers.

Had the Duke of Orleans been protected against himself, he would never have been a rebel; but the King's incomprehensible indulgence transformed into an insurgent a prince who, under any other king, would never have had a guilty thought. "The Duke," Madame Elliott says elsewhere, "was fond of pleasure and detested work and business of any kind; he never read, and devoted himself solely to amusement. At that time he was madly in love with Madame de Buffon, whom he used to take out to drive every day and to the theatre in the evening. It was his misfortune to be surrounded with a troop of ambitious men who gradually used him for their own purposes, and made him see everything in a favorable light, urging him on till he saw himself so far in their power that he could not draw back. . . . I am sure that the Duke had no idea of seizing the throne, whatever may have been the plans of his friends. They expected, I fancy, if they succeeded, to govern him as well as France, and they were capable of any excess in pursuit of their ends."

July 12, 1789, just before the capture of the Bastille, the Duke of Orleans went with Madame Elliott, Prince Louis of Aremberg, and a few other friends, to dine at his castle of Raincy. It was a Sunday. In the morning he had left Paris perfectly calm; on returning in the evening, he heard of all the disorder which had broken out during the day, of the insurrection, with the cries of "Long live the Duke of Orleans!" "Long live Necker!" of the Prince of Lambesc's charge, and of the great agitation of the city and the suburbs. "When I heard of all these things," says Madame Elliott, "I entreated the Duke not to enter Paris in his own carriage. I thought it would be very imprudent for him to appear in the streets at such a moment, and I offered him my carriage. He seemed surprised and much impressed by what had happened in Paris. He hoped, he said, that it would not turn out to be anything serious, and that fear had made my servant exaggerate the truth. . . . I besought the Duke to go at once to Versailles, and not to leave the King so long as Paris was in such disorder. 'If you do this,' I said, 'you will show that the populace made use of your name without your knowledge and consent. You will do well,' I added, 'to tell the King how much you are distressed by all that has happened!'" The Duke gave his word that he would go to Versailles at seven o'clock the next morning; and he did go, but he was not well received. On his arrival he went straight to the King, who had just got out of bed. The King took no notice of him; but since it was the custom that when a prince of the blood was present, that he should give the King his shirt, the gentlemen of the bedchamber handed the shirt to the Duke of Orleans, for him to put it over the King's head. The Duke went up to the King, who asked him what he wanted. The Duke, putting the shirt on the King, answered, "I have come to receive Your Majesty's commands." The King answered very severely, "I have no need of you; go back where you came from."

From that time there was an open feud between the Prince and the court. "From that moment," says Madame Elliott, "I found the Duke much more violent in his political views; and though I never heard him speak otherwise than with respect about the King, I have often heard him speak with great bitterness against the Queen. I was very sorry for it. The court would have done better to remember the Duke's influence, and to hesitate about offending him; for I am very sure that if he had been treated with consideration at that time, and any confidence had been shown him, it would have been possible to get him loose from the dangerous influence of the men who surrounded him."

The lot was thrown. The descendant of Saint Louis and of Henri IV. was about to become a regicide. Verifying by his fate the words of Scripture, that if a house be divided against itself, that house cannot stand, he, like Samson, was to be crushed under the columns he pulled down with his own hands. In less than ten months the scaffold of

Louis XVI. and his own were raised, and he could say, like Macbeth soliloquizing over Duncan's murder: —

> "But here, upon this bank and shoal of time,
> *   *   *   *   *   *
> We still have judgment here; that we but teach
> Bloody instructions, which, being taught, return
> To plague the inventor: this even-handed justice
> Commends the ingredients of our poison'd chalice
> To our own lips."

XXV.

THE BANQUET OF OCTOBER 1.

THURSDAY, October 1, 1789, the theatre of the palace of Versailles was in great commotion; towards four in the afternoon a great banquet was to be given there. At the request of a delegation of the municipality of Versailles, which was alarmed by threats of disorder, the garrison of the town had been strengthened by a regiment from Flanders, which had arrived September 23. An immemorial custom of the French army required that every regiment arriving in a town should be given a dinner of welcome by the other corps. This rule was observed with regard to the regiment from Flanders, and the King's body-guard, who gave the dinner, were authorized to use the palace theatre for this purpose. The officers of the regiment of the Three Bishoprics and those of the National Guard were also invited.

On the stage, which was adorned with scenery representing a forest, was set a table, in the form of a horseshoe, with two hundred plates. In the orchestra were the trumpeters of the body-guard and band of the Flemish regiment. The pit was filled with the men of this regiment and of that of the Three Bishoprics. In the boxes were many spectators, admitted without tickets. The various uniforms, the brilliant lighting, the arrangement of the stage and its decorations, the gorgeous dresses of the ladies, combined to form a most impressive spectacle. At the beginning of the banquet, the feelings that inspired the troops made themselves manifest: the officers swore that they would defend the throne and, if need be, would die for the King; the soldiers expressed the same devotion. It was a festival of honor and fidelity.

A lady of the palace, thinking that such a sight would please and console the royal family, went to the Queen and told her what was going on, advising her to visit the spot with Louis XVI. and the children. The King, who had been hunting in the park of Meudon, entered the palace at that moment. He approved of the plan, and suddenly made his appearance in the royal box with the Queen, his son, and his daughter. The band played the air from "Richard Cœur de Lion": —

"Oh, Richard! oh, my King! the world abandons you";

then the air from the "Deserter": —

"Can one pain what one loves?"

The assembled throng began to cheer; the men waved their hats, the women their handkerchiefs, with the wildest enthusiasm. The royal family left their box and walked through the hall. The Queen, who led her son by his hand, was glad to show him to her faithful servants, whose applause brought tears to her eyes. She remembered the Hungarians who said to her mother, Maria Theresa, *Moriamur pro rege nostro*. Her face, which was generally so sad, was lit up with a ray of happiness. Like Homer's Andromache, she smiled amid her tears.

It was a grand festival, a great manifestation of chivalric honor. It is easy to imagine Marie Antoinette's feelings at finding friends when she thought herself abandoned. Misfortune makes the soul tender and open to impression; the slightest marks of sympathy call forth lively gratitude. How often, when she was living in the fiery furnace of the Revolution, the unhappy Queen must have recalled this last hour of happiness, this last ray of the sun of royalty, gilding the swords that were drawn to express devotion towards her! It is easy to understand the admiration, the ardor, with which the sight of this woman, so noble and so calumniated, must have filled those generous souls! Even now one feels the quiver of enthusiasm, the magnetic current which swept through the hall, and the impression produced on these ardent souls by the sweet and touching melodies which were wonderfully applicable to the circumstances! Grétry, one might almost say, was inspired by prophecy when he gave to Blondel's words an accompaniment so moving and tender. The music admirably expressed the fervor which filled every heart with devotion and loyalty. As for me, when present at the turbulent meetings of the National Assembly, in this same hall which has seen so many vicissitudes, it has happened to me more than once to think, not about the deliberations of the deputies, but of the banquet of October 1, 1789. What I listened to was not the speeches of the orator; no, it was to the distant echo of the band of the Flemish regiment playing that air from "Richard." [1]

The repast, which had been interrupted by the visit of the royal family, was resumed after their departure. When it was over, the guests, the musicians, and the spectators all went into the marble courtyard and began to cheer once more. A soldier of the regiment from Flanders climbed up to the windows of Louis's chamber, to cry, "Long live the King!" close to His Majesty. The festivity continued with serenades and processions until late in the night. These joyous sounds reached the King in his room, and the Queen, tasting a moment of consolation, felt happy in a day of which she did not see the morrow.

The next day the vilest and most shameless calumnies were industriously circulated. The revolutionary pamphleteers resolved to turn the pathetic scene to ridicule, to represent this peaceful entertainment as an orgy, as a terrible debauch. Gorsas, the future Girondist, asserted in the *Courrier de Versailles*, that the health of the nation had been proposed and rejected, and that the drunken guests had trampled

---

[1] A reference to the sessions of the French Chambers held at Versailles for several years after the Franco-Prussian war of 1870–71. — TR.

on the national cockade. Some years later the Queen, before the Revolutionary Tribunal, took pains to refute this absurd calumny. "It is incredible," she said, "that such loyal beings should have been willing to change and trample on a token which the King himself wore."

But hatred found any weapon good to use against Marie Antoinette. The Revolution desired at any price to sully her, because it well knew, as Mirabeau once said, that "the only man the King had about him was the Queen!"

XXVI.

THE FIFTH OF OCTOBER.

MARIE ANTOINETTE'S joy over the evidences of devotion and loyalty which found expression at the banquet of October 1 was destined to be of but brief duration. The next day the wildest calumnies began to circulate once more, and this most generous sovereign was represented as a second Catherine de' Medici, preparing another massacre of Saint Bartholomew. Such ingratitude and malevolence, such a depth of infamy, crushed the unhappy Queen. She, whose character was kind and tender, could not comprehend the malice, cruelty, and degradation of human nature. But her grief was not bitter or noisy; she reflected calmly and seriously, and pardoned everything.

In the morning of October 5, she was in the Little Trianon, long the seat of the rustic pleasures of the royal family. We all know what a melancholy thing it is to revisit in unhappiness places we have known when happy. As Bossuet says: " Already there is a change; the gardens are less rich with flowers, the flowers are less brilliant, their colors less vivid, the meadows less smiling, the water is less clear. . . . The shadow of death is drawing nigh; one perceives the proximity of the fatal gulf. One has to march to the edge. . . . One tries to turn back, but it is impossible; everything has vanished, everything has disappeared."

For some time the Trianon had been deserted. The Queen's last stay there had been from July 15 until August 14, 1788, and since then she had spent only a few hours there, wandering in silent revery beneath the shades which were full of pleasant memories. She was soon to be deprived of the pleasure of looking at the rustic scenery — that last consolation of afflicted hearts. The moment was approaching when she was about to be cast into the Tuileries, her first prison, and when she should be forbidden to revisit the gardens of the Trianon.

It was a dark, rainy day; the whole landscape and the pretty hamlet were gloomy and melancholy. The lawn where charming entertainments used to be given, the trees which in old days had been lit up by fireworks, the Swiss huts where Gessner's idyls and Florian's pastoral had been represented, were now much changed! The willows bending sadly over the lake were real weeping willows. Swans were floating on the water; might one not say that, like the swans of legend, they were about to sing the last song over the death of royalty? The wind roared hoarsely. Poor Queen! The autumn gloom was in full harmony with her spirit; it seemed to weep in sympathy with her. Seated alone, in a grotto, like a statue of Grief, she thought of the sombre present and of the still more sombre future. She watched the leaves fall like the illusions of youth, like glory, like happiness, like power. Everything was full of quiet and melancholy; silence reigned in the deserted garden. She was not to enjoy for long this period of tranquillity. She is interrupted by some one bringing a letter from the Count of Saint Priest, summoning her to return at once to the palace of Versailles.

What had happened? Uneasiness was marked on every face. One of the equerries, M. de Cubières, had hurried off after the King, who was hunting peacefully, and found him at three o'clock near Meudon. Louis XVI. called for his horse, and just when he was placing his foot in the stirrup, a knight of Saint Louis, falling on his knees, said aloud: "Sire, you are deceived; I have just come from the Military School; I have seen nothing but a crowd of women who say they are coming to Versailles to ask for bread. I beg Your Majesty not to be afraid." "Afraid, sir!" the King answered with warmth; "I have never in my life been afraid." Then galloping down one of the steepest slopes in the Meudon forest, he hastened to Versailles, where he found the Queen.

In Paris all day the excitement had been excessive. Women had been running up and down the streets, crying out that there was no more bread at the bakers' shops. They had hastened to the Hôtel de Ville to complain of the authorities. The rioters sounded the tocsin, and Maillard, who had been conspicuous at the capture of the Bastille, had taken a drum and headed the women in their march. Followed by this singular array, he had gone down the quay, passed through the Louvre, the Tuileries, the Champs Élysées, the Cours la Reine, and set out for Versailles. A crowd of idlers, beggars, and thieves followed the band, singing, and shouting jests and appeals for vengeance. They stopped at every wine-shop, and called out to the passers-by and to people at the windows; they were brandishing old muskets and broken swords, dull hatchets, pikes, and rusty daggers.

The weather was very bad; the half-drunken women could hardly walk through the wind. "Austrian," said one of the furies, speaking about Marie Antoinette, "you have danced for your own pleasure; you shall dance for ours. I want your skin to make ribbons of, your blood in my inkstand, my apron for your entrails!" and ferocious jests and insults fell in a perfect shower. Madame Elisabeth, who was at her house in Montreuil, saw from the terrace in her garden, the band marching up the Avenue de Paris. She went at once to the palace of Versailles, and advised her brother to repress the disorder at once. At about half-past three the regiment from Flanders was drawn up in line on the Place d'Armes, to the left of the palace. The body-guard, to the number of about three hundred, was placed before the entrance to the Minister's apartments. A detachment of dragoons was posted in the Avenue de Paris. These were all the forces which the King could dispose of for his defence. Indecision prevailed among the ministers who were in session; M. de Saint Priest wanted the bridge of Sèvres defended, and urged that Louis XVI. go, at the head of his loyal troops, to drive back, at the crossing of the Seine, the body of Parisians of whom, doubtless, the horde of women was the vanguard. But Necker opposed all resistance; he said that if the sword were drawn against the insurrection, it would be the signal for civil war; he preferred treating with the revolt, as from one power to another.

Meanwhile the women had got into the Avenue de Paris, singing, "Long live Henri IV.!" and shouting as if in derision, "Long live the King!" When they reached the Menus Plaisirs, where the National Assembly was sitting, they stopped. At first fifteen of them entered the meeting and were conducted to the bar. Maillard spoke in their name, saying that Paris was without bread, and that some means must be devised for finding a supply. Then the rest of the women crowded into the hall. The galleries, the bar, the deputies' seats, were filled with a noisy, loud-talking multitude, who interrupted the members, insulting those of the right, and fraternizing with those of the left.

The Prince of Luxembourg, a captain of the body-guard, asked Louis XVI. if he had any orders to give about repelling the onslaught. "What, sir," answered the good-natured monarch, "orders to fight women! You are jesting!" The body-guard, which was drawn up ready for action, was forbidden to lay a hand on sabre or pistol. Commands were given to avoid anything that might provoke the populace. The rioters, who kept coming in large numbers, felt confidence in their security. They went up to the gates of the palace, in a rage at finding them closed, and threw stones at the body-guard, who had no cartridges and had been ordered not to defend themselves. At the same time women surrounded the regiment from Flanders and tried to corrupt the men. One of them, Théroigne de Méricourt, who wore a red cloak, went through the ranks, flattering the soldiers and distributing money.

Soon afterwards, Mounier left the National Assembly, followed by a deputation of the women of Paris, whom he led to the palace. The rain was falling in torrents. The Avenue de Paris was filled with a threatening crowd. The rioters in vain tried to force the gates. Only Mounier and the deputation of women were admitted.

The King, who was at the council with his Ministers, went to his bedroom to receive these strange visitors. Only five women were admitted. A young girl of seventeen, named Louise Chabry, spoke for them. "You ought to know my heart," answered the King; "I shall give orders to collect all the bread that can be found." Louise Chabry was so much moved by the King's kindness that she fainted. Louis XVI. made her drink some wine and held salts to her nose. She recovered consciousness, and the King kissed her. The delegates were delighted with the reception accorded them, and went down the marble staircase, shouting, "Long live the King!" and when they saw the other women outside the grating, they said, "We have got what we wanted; we are going back to Paris." These wise words did not please the crowd. Cries arose: "They have sold out to the court! They have received twenty-five louis apiece! To the lantern with them!" They sprang upon the unhappy women, struck them, and tried to hang them. They escaped with difficulty. The disorder increased with every moment. The general alarm, which was beaten in every street, called together the National Guard of Versailles in the Place d'Armes; but many of its members, intimidated by the hostility manifested by certain companies against the body-guard, withdrew.

In the palace, every one was overwhelmed with anxiety. There could be heard the vile abuse poured forth on Marie Antoinette by the frantic crowd. Orders were given to prepare for the departure of the Queen and the Dauphin. The King's carriages left the stables and drove to the door of the Orange house, while the Queen's, starting from the rue de la Pompe at the same time, reached the Dragon's gate. Here a hostile band of the National Guard compelled the coachmen to go back to the stables. Moreover, Marie Antoinette had not been informed of her proposed departure; and on no consideration would she have left the King. Her energetic and haughty nature would have repelled every plan that savored of timidity.

Night was coming on, and the rain continued to fall, exciting hope in the palace that the bad weather would allay the excitement and disperse the rioters. At about eight o'clock in the evening all the troops drawn up in the Place d'Armes received orders to withdraw. The regiment from Flanders left the place, and marched to the courtyard of the Great Stables. The body-guard then proceeded to their quarters, followed by the jeers of the multitude. In the night they left for Trianon, then for Rambouillet. There remained at Versailles only the sentinels on duty, who were to play so tragic a part in the events of the following day.

The town presented a most gloomy and alarming appearance. All the shops, except those of the bakers and a few wine-sellers, were closed. The night was very dark. The inhabitants scarcely dared to set foot out of doors. Ragged men, armed with staves and pikes, knocked at every door, demanding food and drink. The women from Paris continued to fill the National Assembly, which looked like a theatre on a day of free admission. They sent out for bread, wine, and meat, and ate and slept on the benches of the deputies. A certain number of the representatives remained in the hall; and in Mounier's absence, the President's chair was taken by the Bishop of Langres, who, in spite of his ecclesiastical dignity, had to submit to being kissed by a number of women more or less drunk. Suddenly, towards midnight, a great piece of news spread: the National Guard of Paris and its commander, La Fayette, had just arrived in Versailles.

Ever since morning La Fayette had been the prey of the keenest anguish. At daybreak a number of battalions had surrounded the Hôtel de Ville, and instead of trying to quell the outbreak, had been themselves shouting all day long, "To Versailles, to Versailles!" La Fayette hesitated. Should he obey the demands of his mutinous soldiers, or should he, as it were, sanctify the rebellion by his presence? Should he, by resistance, compromise the popularity which he had acquired by so many sacrifices? "It is singular," exclaimed one of the National Guard, "that M. de La Fayette should think of commanding the people, when in fact it is the people who command him." Cries for blood and accusations of treachery began to be heard.

The Commune at last gave the National Guard orders to start. It was six in the morning. La Fayette was on horseback, his head bowed, his heart full of gloomy forebodings, and after a few moments' hesitation he made up his mind, and as if urged by a power he could not resist, he shouted, "Forward, march!"

The lot was thrown. Twenty thousand men

marched forth. The vanguard consisted of three companies of grenadiers, a battalion of fusiliers, and three cannon. Seven or eight hundred men, bare-armed, and hoarse with drink, followed, carrying staves or pikes. Then came La Fayette, the servant rather than the commander of his troops. An aide galloped ahead to announce to the King the advance of the National Guard; he reached Versailles at about ten in the evening, and found the whole court in alarm. The Queen alone was undaunted; during the evening she had been receiving a number of people and had talked with energy and dignity, giving strength to others by her calm and courage.

Towards midnight the National Guard of Paris reached the gates of Versailles. Before entering the town, La Fayette stopped a moment and administered to his troops the oath of loyalty to the nation, the laws, and the King. Then he entered the Avenue de Paris, in which was the hall where the National Assembly met, and assured the President of the pacific intentions of his troops. Then leaving the Assembly, he betook himself to the palace, which he entered with only two members of the municipal government of Paris. The rooms were crowded; a voice shouted, "There's Cromwell!"

"Sir," answered La Fayette, "Cromwell would not have come alone."

The court was in doubt whether the man who came in this way was a liberator or a tyrant, whether he came to save or to overthrow the King. La Fayette advanced in an attitude of grief and respect. He bowed low before Louis XVI., and said, "Sire, I have come to bring you my head to save Your Majesty's." And he added that he felt confident of the sentiments of the National Guard. Louis XVI., who was hopeful by nature, believed La Fayette, who, for his part, meant what he said. It was agreed that the interior of the palace should be left in charge of the sentinels on duty, and that the National Guard should take charge of the outside. La Fayette went out to see about carrying out this order. Then he returned to the Assembly which, in a night session, was discussing a proposed penal law. He said that he would be responsible for everything, and that order would be maintained.

President Mounier, satisfied with this optimistic utterance, adjourned the session at three in the morning, and La Fayette went back to the palace, where he heard that the King had gone to bed, and that all was quiet. Then he mounted his horse and rode through the town, which was perfectly calm. He then went back to the palace and stayed there, in the rooms of M. Montmorin, until six the next morning, when, utterly exhausted, after being on horseback for seventeen hours, repose was necessary. After a last look at the town he went to the house belonging to his wife's family, in the rue de la Pompe, and lay down on a bed. His sleep, which lasted only a few moments, has been the subject of severe condemnation from historians.

XXVII.

THE SIXTH OF OCTOBER.

VERSAILLES was at last finding rest: the royal family in the palace; La Fayette in the Noailles mansion; the National Guard of Paris, wet through with the rain, and worn out by a march to which it was not accustomed, in the churches, the quarters of the body-guard, and in private houses; the women and the men, with pikes, on the benches of the National Assembly, in the barracks of the French Guards, and the wine-shops. Those of the populace who had no refuge had lit a large fire in the Place d'Armes, and after cutting up and roasting a wounded horse, had quietly fallen asleep in this improvised bivouac.

Marie Antoinette, worn out by the emotions of this painful day, had gone to bed at two in the morning. Before she went to sleep, she had told the two ladies of her bedchamber, Madame Auguié and Madame Thibaut, to go to their beds, thinking that for this night, at least, there was nothing to fear. She owed her life the next day to the devotion which prevented these two ladies from obeying this command.

All the lights were out, and Marie Antoinette was

sound asleep. The sleep which precedes a battle or a riot is an imposing thing, in the contrast that exists between its calm and the excitement and danger of the next day; for many it is the last sleep of their lives, a prelude to the sleep of death, and there is something most impressive in its mysteriousness. It is like a heaven-sent truce.

Not every one in Versailles enjoyed this truce in the night between the 5th and 6th of October. Everything was at rest, except crime. The revolt had not yet completed its task; and these demons, these disguised brigands, who were shouting for bread when their pockets were full of gold, had not yet earned their pay. No, there was no sleep — for hate knows no fatigue — for the furies who had sworn to cut off Marie Antoinette's neck on a milestone, and to dip their hands in her blood. At the Assembly, one wild-eyed woman had asked, with threatening gestures, brandishing a dagger, if the Austrian woman's apartments were well guarded.

That evening the men with pikes had made a great tumult in the Place d'Armes, shouting to the respectable people who tried to quiet them, "Go to bed; as for us, we haven't finished our work." They were waiting for daylight.

Let us, in company with M. Le Roi, a learned guide, a real student, examine the scene of the events which were about to take place.[1] Let us first look at

---

[1] *History of Versailles: its Streets, Squares and Avenues from the Origin of the City to the Present Time.*

the palace, as well as at all the gratings of the entrances which had been closed on the 5th of October, and had kept out the populace, but, the next day, was to give free passage to the rioters.

At the present day we can pass through the wide gateway opening on the Place d'Armes, and enter at once the huge courtyard which extends to the palace.

In the reign of Louis XVI. there was, in addition, a second grating between the two wings of the palace, just about where now stands the equestrian statue of Louis XIV.

The space between the two gratings was called the Ministers' Courtyard, from the buildings on each side in which the ministers lodged.

Then, as now, there was an iron gate opening on the rue des Reservoirs, and another opening on the rue de la Surintendance (now the rue de la Bibliothèque).

Beyond the courtyard of the Ministers was the Royal Courtyard, extending to the narrow space between the old buildings of the palace of Louis XIII., then, as now, called the Marble Courtyard, from the pavement.

Let us first notice the insufficiency of La Fayette's defensive measures, and the absence of any excuse for his fatal confidence. During the whole of the 5th, the gateway of the Ministers' Courtyard was the point attacked by the populace, furious at finding this barrier. Well! Who guarded this gate which was of such importance for the defence of the palace? Two soldiers of the National Guard! Who protected the entrance of the marble staircase leading to the royal apartments? Two Swiss soldiers! Why was it that the royal battalions of the National Guard, which certainly contained trusty men, were not ordered to defend the approaches to the palace?

Why was it that their commander, instead of going to rest in the rue de la Pompe, did not stay in the palace, near his King, at the post of duty and of honor? Without doubt, La Fayette was no traitor; but, like men of his political complexion, he was absurdly optimistic, and he did not dread the danger which lay before his eyes. He lay down in good faith, and when he awoke from his short sleep, he was overcome with surprise at events which any one else would have foreseen.

At half-past five in the morning, a great number of women suddenly made their appearance in the Place d'Armes. Many of them went up to the first gateway, that leading to the Ministers' Courtyard, and the two National Guards who were stationed there opened the gate. The men, armed with pikes, at once followed, and the courtyard was filled. The crowd saw that the gate of the Princes' Courtyard (the one leading to the middle of the palace, where dwelt the princes of the blood) was open, and the populace hastened thither, and entered the park by a door at the foot of the princes' staircase. At that moment, Marie Antoinette was awakened by the noise beneath her windows. She rang for Madame

Thibaut, and asked the meaning of this tumult. Madame Thibaut replied that it was the women from Paris, who, probably, not being able to find any quarters, were walking on the terrace. Then she withdrew; and the Queen, satisfied, remained in bed.

The Royal Court was still secure. The mayor of the body-guard, M. d'Aguesseau, had just placed many guards in the passage of the colonnade leading from the Princes' Courtyard to the Royal Courtyard; but those soldiers were too few to make any resistance, and the wave of rioters drove them back; the Royal Courtyard was invaded; one of the body-guard, a man named Deshuttes, was disarmed in front of the gateway, struck down, and dragged, dying, to the end of the Ministers' Courtyard. A ragpicker named Jourdan placed his foot on his chest, and cut off his head with an axe. This head was stuck on the point of a pike, and paraded through the streets as a trophy of the insurrection, and the victim's body was carried to the barracks of the French Guard, and thrown on the straw.

At the same time, the crowd made a violent attack on the marble staircase, which is near the Marble Courtyard, and led to the apartments of the King and Queen. At the top, facing the staircase, was the great hall of the Guards. To the left, a landing led to the hall of the King's Guards; then came the King's ante-chamber, then the hall of the Œil de Bœuf, then the bedroom of Louis XIV., the Ministers' Council Hall; and finally, at the right of this hall, the bedroom of Louis XVI.

On the right of the marble staircase was a door leading to Marie Antoinette's apartments: first, is the hall of the Guards; the first ante-chamber, called also the drawing-room of the Grand Couvert; the second ante-chamber, called the Queen's drawing-room; then her bedroom.

The marble staircase was defended by only two men of the Hundred Swiss Guards. The crowd mounted the staircase, and one of the body-guard, M. Miomandre de Sainte-Marie, went down three or four steps, saying, "My friends, you love your King, and you come to disturb him in his palace." The rioters sprang on this loyal servant, and nearly killed him. Then the body-guards, seeing that they could not withstand the onslaught, took refuge, some in the great hall of the Guards, the others in the hall of the King's Guards. At the same moment the door between the marble staircase and the hall of the Queen's Guards was burst open, and the rioters rushed in, calling for the death of Marie Antoinette. One of the guards on duty as sentinel before the door of the first ante-chamber, M. de Varicourt, was struck from behind, and fell bleeding; the crowd seized him, hustled him down the staircase, and dragged him through the Princes' Gate into the Ministers' Courtyard. He was still living, and struggling with his assassins, when Jourdan, the ragpicker, ran up, and with his axe, still dripping with the blood of M. Deshuttes, cut off his head.

Another one of the guard, M. du Repaire, took M.

de Varicourt's place at the entrance of the first antechamber. They rushed upon him; but after a long struggle, he managed to reach the hall of the King's Guards, covered with wounds; just as the door closed behind him, a pistol-shot laid low one of the assailants. M. Miomandre de Sainte-Marie, who had sought refuge in the embrasure of one of the windows of the great hall of the Guards, hastened to take M. de Varicourt's place in the hall of the Queen's Guards, at the door of the first ante-chamber. He opened the door quickly and saw Madame Thibaut; to her he said, "Save the Queen; they want to kill her." Then he closed the door, and the two ladies of the bedchamber, Madame Thibaut and Madame Auguié, who were in the Queen's drawing-room, bolted it. Then the wretches attacked M. Miomandre de Sainte-Marie. One of them felled him, bleeding, to the ground with the butt-end of a musket. They thought he was killed, and stole his watch; then they hastened to the great hall to seize the weapons of the body-guard. M. de Sainte-Marie came to himself and saw that he was alone; he dragged himself to the landing and made his way to his companions in the hall of the King's Guards.

Meanwhile Madame Thibaut had made the Queen get up and hurried her into her stockings and petticoat, and thrown a cloak over her shoulders. At the end of the bedroom, near the bed, was a secret door, opening on a dark passage-way, which led to the hall of the Œil de Bœuf. At the entrance of this passage-way was a little staircase leading to a passage known as the King's passage-way, which communicated with the King's bedroom, enabling him thus to go to the Queen's room unobserved. Marie Antoinette, accompanied by the two ladies of her bedchamber, passed out through the door at the foot of her bed, made her way to the passage leading to the Œil de Bœuf, and knocked at the door there, which was opened by the footmen of Louis XVI., and entered the King's apartment.

At the same time Louis XVI., full of anxiety for his wife and children, had wanted to go to the Queen. He had taken the other passage-way, and reached her room just as she had left it. The guards told him, and he returned the same way to his own chamber, where he found the Queen and the Dauphin, who had just been brought by Madame de Tourzel, the governess of the royal children.

Meanwhile the National Guard began to enter the palace; the first to arrive was a detachment that had passed the night in the Church of the Franciscans; it ascended the staircase and rescued the members of the body-guard who had sought refuge in the hall of the Œil de Bœuf.

After a few moments' sleep, of which it will be said that "he slept just long enough to ruin the King," La Fayette woke up in the Noailles mansion. He did not wait for a horse to be brought, but started at once for the palace on foot, and proceeded to encourage his men to quell the disorder. Louis XVI.

himself thanked the members of the National Guard who had saved the lives of his body-guard; then, always calm and self-controlled, he called the ministers together in the Council Hall. The Queen, the Dauphin, Madame Royale, Madame Elisabeth, the Count of Provence, the aunts, were all collected in the King's bedroom. The Dauphin said to his mother, "Mamma, I'm hungry." "Be patient," answered Marie Antoinette; "this will soon be over."

The palace courtyards were filled with battalions of the National Guard and with the populace. Marie Antoinette stood, perfectly calm, at a window, looking out on the vast throng. While every one about her was giving way to tears or despair, she did not lose her head for a moment, but consoled and encouraged every one.

Louis XVI. went out on the balcony, with the same air of confidence and kindness that he always wore. Cries of "The Queen, the Queen!" were heard. La Fayette advised Marie Antoinette to show herself; he said it was the only way to allay the excitement. "Very well," answered the Queen, "if I have to go to my execution, I shall not hesitate; I will go." What was to take place? What was to be expected of these men, drunk, and wild with wrath, uttering angry cries and carrying loaded muskets? Would the assassins of the body-guard hesitate at the murder of a woman, a queen? It was a solemn moment. Marie Antoinette, pale, with dishevelled hair, appeared at the balcony of the King's room, accompanied by La Fayette, and holding the Dauphin with one hand, her daughter with the other. The cries redoubled; shouts of "No children! No children! The Queen alone!" arose from all sides. What did this uproar mean? Did the demons who filled the place fear that the sight of the children would touch their hearts? Did the murderers who would gladly have slain the mother hesitate about killing a boy and a girl? Without thinking about the probable evil significance of these shouts, Marie Antoinette gave the Dauphin and his sister to their father; then she came out alone, fearless, heroic, and calmly letting her eyes run over the multitude, folded her arms.

It was the daughter of the Cæsars who appeared. The noble haughtiness of her brow, the dignity of her bearing, wrung from the crowd a shout of admiration and surprise. Even those who, a moment before, wanted to kill her, joined in the cry. A loud roar of "Long live the Queen!" burst forth. Marie Antoinette was not the dupe of this greeting; she heard the crowd shouting another alarming cry: "To Paris with the King!" and, leaving the balcony, she went up to Madame Necker, and said sadly, "They are going to make the King and me go to Paris, with the heads of our guards carried before us on the ends of their pikes."

Louis XVI., always weakly good-natured, decided to obey this insolent demand of the populace. All that he asked was that he should not be separated from his wife and children. La Fayette went out on the balcony with one of the body-guard, and made him take an oath of fidelity to the nation and show the side of his hat on which was fastened the tricolor cockade. The other guards followed this example. The grenadiers of the National Guard put their hats on the end of their bayonets, and every one shouted, "Long live the body-guard!"

At the same time letters were thrown from the palace windows, announcing that the King was going to leave for Paris, and the National Guard gave expression to its delight by firing many rounds of musketry. When the Assembly heard the news, it passed a vote, on the motion of Mirabeau, that it could not be separated from the King. Louis XVI., when the vote was communicated to him, said: "It is with sincere emotion that I receive this new proof of the attachment of the Assembly. The wish of my heart, as you know, is never to be separated from you. I am going to Paris with the Queen and my children. I shall give all necessary orders for the continuation of the Assembly's work."

The preparations for the departure of the royal family were speedily completed. The King, the Queen, Madame Elisabeth, the Dauphin, the King's brother, Madame Royale, and Madame Tourzel, all got into the same carriage. It was one o'clock in the afternoon.

Such are vicissitudes of fate! It was there on the balcony of the great King's chamber, that absolute monarchy expired, that divine right of which he was the proudest representative! Such the mutability of life! It is this Place d'Armes, where used to be deployed the military splendor and the royal pomp, that had become the scene of the last humiliations of royalty! The proud river was ending in sand.

It was all over; Louis XVI. and Marie Antoinette were departing, never to return. Farewell, Versailles! Farewell to the magnificent palace with its bright galleries and solemn chapel! Farewell to the park, to its statues, to its mighty trees! The King and the Queen were vanquished, and never was the Revolution to let them see again their former palace. All that was to be allowed them was to see its towers in the distance, as if it were an Eden from which they had been driven, not by angels, but by devils.

The procession started. The van consisted of the men and women who had left Paris the evening before. The women wore the tricolor cockades in their caps; the men waved in triumph the arms they had captured from the body-guard. A great many of the rioters were in cabs; others in carts, or riding on the cannon. Then followed sixty wagons filled with flour taken from the market in Versailles. Women, carrying branches, shouted out, "We are bringing the baker, the baker's wife, and the baker's little boy."

After the wagons came the battalions of the National Guard, surrounded by the populace; then the body-guard, disarmed, humiliated, with torn uniforms, like captives in ancient triumphs, tokens of the victory of the insurrection; then the large carriage containing the royal family: La Fayette and M. d'Estaing, the commander of the National Guard of Versailles, rode, one on each side of the carriage. A noisy crowd clung close to the carriage. There were but few cries of "Long live the King!" Everywhere rose shouts of "Long live the Nation! Down with the black caps! To the lantern with the bishops!" As if in mockery, a magnificent sun shone on this funeral procession of royalty. The weather, which had been abominable the day before, was delightful on that day. While authority, discipline, honor, everything that makes a nation's power and glory, had been insulted in the person of the son of Saint Louis, of Henri IV., of Louis XIV., the autumn was glowing with its last splendor, the birds were singing in the woods of Viroflay. The majesty of nature seemed to protest by its calm against human agitation and folly.

After a journey of seven hours, the royal family was to sleep that night in Paris, in its palace, or rather in its prison. The drama of Versailles was over; the drama of the Tuileries was beginning.

EPILOGUE.

VERSAILLES SINCE 1789.

AT Versailles, the morning of October 6, 1789, everything was noise, tumult, and excitement; that evening all was peace and silence. The town, wearied by what it had gone through, was sadly resting. The palace was deserted. A few enthusiastic demagogues only seemed happy. The vast majority of the inhabitants foresaw the future, and understood that the departure of the King meant the ruin of Versailles. This town, once so brilliant, sank into gloom, and its population diminished; widowed of the court, it wore a sombre aspect. A Russian traveller who visited it in 1790 was struck by its desolation. He says that he had to wait two hours for a wretched meal, and that then his hostess said to him, "These are hard times, sir; everybody is suffering, and you must have your share." He adds that in the trees of Trianon, "the birds still sing their love-songs; they sing, but, alas, no longer in the presence of kings! No one listens to them except a few foreigners who come to the park to meditate."

The Revolution bore an especial grudge against

the former sanctuary of the monarchy. Vandalism was more common there than anywhere else. October 20, 1792, Roland sent to the Convention a letter requesting permission to sell the furniture of the palace. The deputy Manual proposed, in addition, placing a sign on the palace, bearing these words: "This house for sale or to let." The Convention authorized the sale of the furniture, and referred the other proposition to a committee. In 1794, the administration of the district of Versailles "informs its fellow-citizens that the Little Trianon, which has too long been withheld from agriculture, and devoted to the luxury of tyrants and their lackeys, a constant insult to the misery of the people, is about to be restored to cultivation." The eighteen acres of the little park had been already divided into ten lots, and it was only by the merest chance that the work of destruction was not completed. The park still exists; but what has become of the Little Trianon palace, that pretty temple of which Marie Antoinette was the deity? The drawing-room furniture, in blue silk, stuffed with eiderdown, the bed covered with white silk lace, the curtains fastened with pearls and Grenada silk, — all that was for sale for four hundred thousand francs at a second-hand shop in rue Neuve de l'Egalité. The rooms smelt like a cellar; the little lake was a swamp; the village a ruin.

And the famous palace of Versailles, so long the symbol of power and glory, alas! how it changed! Versailles without courtiers was like a church without priests, or barracks without soldiers. Everything began to go to ruin, — the rooms, the marble statues, the bronze groups. A few beggars, former servants of the best of masters, pursued the visitors in hope of alms. As Volney said in his *Ruins:* "A busy crowd once thronged these now deserted paths; within these walls, where all is silence, sounded the hum of work, and sounds of joy and merrymaking. A mysterious Providence administers incomprehensible judgment. Doubtless he afflicts the earth with a secret curse, and in vengeance of races that are passed, he has smitten those of the present. Oh! who will undertake to fathom the wonders of the Divine Being?"

It was a singular irony of fate: in 1797, the keeper of a coffee-house at Versailles rented the Little Trianon, and opened there a restaurant and public ball-room; there the crowd played, smoked, and danced, indulging in ribald talk, and drinking more or less adulterated wine in this once most aristocratic spot, the former home of every luxury. In 1800, a branch of the Hôtel des Invalides was installed in the palace of Versailles. Two thousand veterans were established in the central wing and in the apartments of Louis XV. and Louis XVI. Not even the chambers of the kings inspired respect.

During the First Empire the palaces of Versailles and those of Trianon had a few hours of glory. January 3, 1805, the town was visited by Pius VII., who came for the coronation of the man who was then called a second Constantine, and he desired to see the palace of the old monarchy. He left Paris in a carriage drawn by eight horses and escorted by men of the Imperial Guard, to make his formal entrance into Versailles. Amid the roar of artillery and the ringing of all the church bells, he went first to the cathedral and then to the palace. After letting more than five hundred people kiss his ring, in the grand apartments and the Gallery of the Mirrors, he went out on the balcony, in the middle of the gallery, looking out on the park. An immense multitude was on the terrace, impatiently waiting for the Vicar of Christ to appear.

As soon as the Holy Father came out on the balcony, the whole crowd fell on their knees, bareheaded. And this same people who, less than ten years before, was guillotining the priests, breaking the sacred vessels, and had installed a prostitute on the high altar of Notre Dame of Paris, now knelt in repentance to receive the blessing of this venerable man who brought to France the word of peace and the pardon of the God of pity. With more truth than the Doge of Venice, the Pope might have answered the question, what most surprised him at Versailles, "It is to see myself here." It was a happy moment for the Church, for France, and for Napoleon. The Holy Father, surprised and touched, exclaimed with deep emotion, "Is this the French people who are called so irreligious?"

In 1805, the Emperor gave orders for the restoration of the palaces of Versailles and Trianon, which had reverted to the crown. February 5, a ball was given in the Hercules drawing-room. The haughty upstart moved as a conqueror in the palace of kings; and in spite of his wonderful fortune, he, the son of a poor and obscure Corsican gentleman, must have felt surprise at being master of the Sun King's palace. The conqueror's court was then most brilliant, and the glow of victory lit up all the residences of this man of destiny. He sought at the Grand Trianon a few moments' peace in the mournful moments of his varied career. This was December 16, 1809, the day when he divorced the Empress Josephine, the loved companion of his happy days. He, man of action, of iron, as he was, this giant of battles, was not so void of feeling as some have supposed. He suffered all the sufferings of the woman he had once loved so dearly; and, thinking in turn of her and of Marie Antoinette, during the week he spent at Trianon after the divorce, he doubtless said more than once that the royal or imperial crown often turns into a crown of thorns, in a country torn and troubled like ours.

July 10, 1811, the Emperor came again to Trianon, and this time in company with the Empress Marie Louise. August 25, on her birthday, after a performance in the theatre of the Little Trianon, the gardens were illuminated as in the time of Marie Antoinette. The Emperor walked through them, hat in hand, with the Empress on his arm, and the whole court following them. He went first to the Temple of Love; then to the hamlet, where had been arranged a number of scenes of rustic life, and where a Flemish picture was represented in action; and finally, to the octagon pavilion, where musicians performed a cantata. The entertainment closed with a grand ball in the gallery of the Great Trianon. In 1813, the Emperor resided there from the 7th to the 22d of March with the Empress Marie Louise and Queen Hortense, and it is there that he wrote a letter of advice and friendliness to Josephine. It is there, too, that he collected a library of more than two thousand volumes, consisting of the masterpieces of human intelligence. He remembered this library after his second abdication; and he asked the Chamber of Deputies for permission to carry these books with him into exile, hoping to get from them some comfort for his cruel griefs. The Chamber, by a unanimous vote, acceded to the desire of the man who, a short time before, had disposed of the sceptres and crowns of Europe. But the wish of the fallen sovereign could not be carried out: foreign troops had sacked and pillaged Napoleon's library.

Louis XVIII. seldom visited Versailles; the palace in which he had dwelt in his youth was full of sad memories. The arrangement of the halls and room had not been changed; and Louis XVIII. was able to distinguish all the rooms in the central wing in which he had lived when Count of Provence. Charles X. also went very seldom to Versailles. In 1830, when he was dethroned, he stopped for a moment at Trianon. It was the first station of his exile.

Louis Philippe, who, in spite of the democratic origin of the royalty of July, had aristocratic tastes, and who would have liked nothing better than to be, if the Revolution had permitted, a sovereign like Louis XIV., took much more interest in Versailles than Louis XVIII. or Charles X. He obtained from the Chambers money enough for the restoration of the palace, but only on the condition of establishing there a historical museum. The Versailles of the Sun King was put under the protection of the Republic, of the Empire, and of the Monarchy of 1830. That was the only way to avoid wounding the passions and susceptibilities of the time. The glories of the old régime were obliged to seek protection from the toleration of the new.

The creation of the Versailles Museum had been decreed September 1, 1833; it was inaugurated June 10, 1837. A grand state dinner, at which Louis Philippe presided, was given in the Gallery of the Mirrors. At the King's table were laid six hundred plates. After the dinner, the royal family and all the guests went into the theatre; this hall, which had been richly decorated, was all ablaze with light. Mademoiselle Mars and the principal actors of the Comédie Française played "Le Misanthrope." Then Duprez, Levasseur, and Mademoiselle Falcon sang selections from the third and fifth acts of "Robert le Diable." "The performance," we read in the

Moniteur of June 12, 1837, "terminated with an interlude by M. Scribe, intended to celebrate the inauguration of the Museum, and to compare an entertainment given at Versailles by Louis XIV. with the wholly national festival given this day by the King of the French. The company was filled with the liveliest enthusiasm at the moment when the art of the decorator made the view of the old Versailles follow that of Versailles restored to its former glory, and consecrated by Louis Philippe to the arts that honor the country."

After the performance, the King and the guests went through all the halls of the palace and the new gallery, the Gallery of the Battles, "where one sees traced on canvas," says the *Moniteur*, "all the great exploits of French valor, from the battle of Tolbiac to that of Wagram." This promenade with torches was very impressive. Footmen in red livery went before the King, carrying torches. Louis Philippe was very proud of his triumph.

October 17, 1837, in the chapel of Trianon, was celebrated the marriage of Princess Marie of Orleans — who made the statue of Joan of Arc — with Duke Alexander of Würtemberg. The Little Trianon was the summer residence of the Duke and Duchess of Orleans.

Charles X., before leaving for foreign parts, rested a moment at Trianon, July 31, 1830. February 24, 1848, another exile also stopped there: this exile was Louis Philippe. The law of revenge was applied.

The younger branch endured the same fate as the elder one. In our century of revolutions, are not palaces like inns, in which sovereigns, like travellers, merely pass through; and cannot the exile of the day repeat to the exile of the morrow this motto of the cemetery: *Hodie mihi, cras tibi?*

April 22, 1849, the heir of Napoleon, who had become the President of the French Republic, held a review on the Place d'Armes, and before the statue of Louis XIV. he presented banners to the battalions of the National Guard of Seine-et-Oise.

February 1, 1853, a bridegroom with a woman of rare beauty by his side entered the palace courtyard at Versailles, in a tilbury which he drove himself. As soon as the wagon stopped, the Curator of the Museum was summoned by the couple, who asked him to show them all the portraits of Marie Antoinette there were in the palace. M. Soulié hastened to comply with their desire. Before him stood the man who, on the previous evening, had worn the collar of the Legion of Honor which Napoleon I. had worn at his coronation, and the very golden fleece of the Emperor Charles V.; the woman, full of grace and charm, in her long dress of white silk, her diadem and waistband of diamonds, her white veil adorned with orange-flowers, had drawn from the numberless crowd exclamations of surprise, joy, and admiration. Now, she was in simple walking-dress, without maid-of-honor, or escort of any kind. But in her mind, in her eyes, still lingered that vision of the previous evening, — the Élysée, the Tuileries, the Place du Louvre, the rue de Rivoli, the quays, all decorated with poles, pennants, awnings, and inscriptions; the women waving their handkerchiefs and throwing bouquets; the soldiers and the National Guard saluting; the dashing regiment of the Guards; the light cavalry in their golden cuirasses; the deputations of workingmen, with their banners in front; the old soldiers of the First Empire, the veterans of Austerlitz, Jena, and Wagram; the young girls in white; then the towers of Notre Dame upholding four eagles and two huge tricolored flags; the entrance of this old cathedral, with its tapestries representing equestrian statues of Charlemagne and Napoleon, and, beneath the vaulted roof of the church, the banners of the eighty-six departments of France; the fifteen thousand candles lighting the nave; the high altar, resplendent with lights and flowers. All this the Empress still had in her eyes, and in her ears still resounded the cannon of the Invalides, the roll of the drums, the sound of trumpets and church bells, the enthusiastic applause of the people, the songs of the Church, the majestic roar of the organ. She still breathed the heavy perfume of the incense; she heard the echo of the litanies, and of the hosannas, and yet she was sad. In spite of this apotheosis, the glory of which still dazzled her, at this moment when she thought herself the dupe of a dream, her mind was anxious and troubled; her soul was filled, not with pride, but with melancholy.

Doubtless, too, she remembered that another woman, another sovereign, had, too, been exalted, flattered, half deified; and as she thought of that woman, she recalled no longer the triumphal march of the previous evening, but those three stopping-places of the other, — the Temple, the Conciergerie, the Place Louis XV. The Emperor seemed full of confidence in the future: never had his faith in his star seemed firmer; it manifested itself in every sentence, in every word of the speech he uttered before the great bodies of the State, in the Tuileries, January 23, 1853, announcing that great bit of news, his marriage. He then said: "I have preferred a woman whom I love and whom I respect, to any unknown woman, alliance with whom would have brought advantages mingled with sacrifices. Without expressing contempt for any one, I follow my inclinations, but after consulting my reason and my convictions. By placing independence, the qualities of the heart, and family happiness above dynastic prejudices and ambitious calculations, I shall not be less strong, since I shall enjoy more freedom." He had also said: "The examples of the past have left behind them in the popular mind a host of superstitious beliefs. It has not forgotten that for sixty years no foreign princess has ascended the steps of the throne without seeing her family scattered and proscribed by war and revolution."

War and revolution! The Emperor was then very sure that he and his wife would never be their victims. The evening before, just when she was finishing her dressing at the Élysée, before going to the Tuileries and to Notre Dame, the Empress had put about her neck a magnificent necklace of pearls. Then an old Spanish servant who was there could not keep from crying out: "Oh, Madame! I beg of you, don't put on that necklace; I am afraid of it. You know what they say at home: 'The more pearls you wear on your wedding-day, the more tears you will shed the rest of your life!'" Nevertheless, the Empress kept on the necklace; but the servant's words had struck her. She heard their distant echo like the sound of an alarm-bell, and, thinking of the tears shed by Marie Antoinette, she said to herself that possibly her eyes, too, would be swollen and scalded with tears. She gazed for a long time, with curiosity mingled with respect and emotion, at the five portraits of the martyred Queen, two of which were painted by the Swedish artist, Roslin, and three by Madame Vigée-Lebrun. One of these portraits hangs in the Queen's chamber, just where her alcove was, to the left, above the little door through which she fled from the assassins in the morning of October 6, 1789.

Another canvas, painted by the same artist, which hangs in the story above, represents Marie Antoinette, in 1787, surrounded by her children, the first Dauphin; the Duke of Normandy, the future Louis XVII.; Madame Royale, the future orphan of the Temple. The Empress stood long in silent revery before this pathetic picture, so crowded with presentiments.

Very near that is another, before which the Emperor doubtless did not stop; but it contains a still gloomier omen. It represents King Jerome, seated by the side of his wife, the Princess Catherine of Würtemberg. The King and Queen of Westphalia are on the terrace of a castle which overlooks a beautiful park, and one sees in the distance a cascade like that of Saint Cloud. This castle Napoleon III. was one day to inhabit. It is his future prison, — Wilhelmshöhe! How fortunate it is for us all, sovereigns or citizens, that we do not know beforehand the fate that awaits us!

But the day of sorrow and mourning was still distant. The Empire which was doomed to such a terrible end had still many years of strength and glory before it.

August 21, 1855, Versailles was in festal array. At the entrance of the Avenue Saint Cloud stood a triumphal arch decorated with the united flags of France and England. On the pediment were inscribed, towards the Avenue of Picardy, the names Victoria and Prince Albert; towards the city the names Napoleon and Eugénie. The Emperor and the Empress went to do the honors of the palace of Louis XIV. to the Queen of England and the Prince Consort.

Towards eleven in the morning, the imperial and royal procession, consisting of a number of carriages drawn by six horses, preceded and followed by an escort of light cavalry, entered the city, stopped for a few moments beneath the triumphal arch to hear the address of welcome of the mayor of Versailles, and then continued its march to the palace, amid the cheers of an enthusiastic crowd.

Four days later, August 25, the Emperor gave a ball in the palace to Queen Victoria. The courtyards and the park were illuminated. Never had the residence of the Sun King been more brilliant. Its majestic architecture shone forth in lines of fire. The sovereigns entered by the marble staircase; the guests, by the princes' stairway. Waiting and resting rooms, boudoirs lined with blue damask and filled with baskets of flowers, had been arranged for the Queen in the apartments of Marie Antoinette. The Gallery of Mirrors was most radiant.

Thousands of lamps and chandeliers cast their light on the jewels and rich dresses. Every window showed a fairy-like sight, the park being no less brilliant than the palace; the great sheet of water, surrounded on all sides by a series of Renaissance porticos, was lit by many-colored lanterns, fastened on trellis work as green as an emerald, and the whole stood out vividly against the trees of the background. In the middle rose a triumphal arch on the top of which appeared the arms of France and of England. On the porticos to the right and the left glittered the initials of the sovereigns; the water arose in slender jets to fall down the cascades beneath bright arches;

the two basins formed a glowing sheet, on which swam golden dolphins, carrying cupids that bore Venetian garlands. At ten o'clock the doors of the grand apartments opened, and Their Majesties entered the Gallery of Mirrors — Queen Victoria on the Emperor's arm; the Empress on that of Prince Albert.

A few moments after began the fireworks, which were set off at the end of the Swiss basin: the principal piece represented Windsor Castle. Then Napoleon III. opened the ball with the Queen. At eleven the sovereigns made their way through the grand apartments of Louis XIV. to the theatre, where supper was served. The table of Their Majesties had been placed in one of the principal boxes overlooking the orchestra and the pit, which had been transformed into a banquet hall. Never was there a more sumptuous festival. The Emperor was then young, triumphant, and full of confidence in himself and his destiny, had no suspicion of the catastrophes hid in the gloomy future, or of the very different festival which was to be celebrated fifteen years later in this same Gallery of the Mirrors, when, at the end of the Crimean War, Imperial France rivalled in splendor the France of the Great King.

January 8, 1871, an altar covered with a red cloth was raised in this gallery, opposite the windows looking out upon the park. On this red cloth was the figure of the Iron Cross of Prussia. Around the altar stood officers holding flags. At one in the afternoon, King William, surrounded by representatives of all the reigning families of Germany, by the members of his family, his generals, and his ministers, entered and took his place before the altar. On his left was noticed Bismarck, who had just been appointed division-commander. A choir of soldiers sang a psalm. The new German Empire was about to be established. After the psalm, the King placed upon the flag the charter of the Empire and bade the Chancellor to read the proclamation to the German people. The new Cæsar announced that, in accordance with the demand of the Princes and the Free Cities, he felt it his duty to restore the Imperial crown and to assume it himself. As soon as the reading of the proclamation was over, the Grand Duke of Baden shouted, "Long live the Emperor of Germany!" The whole assembled company repeated this cry three times; then the bands played the Prussian national hymn. The gray light of a winter day lit up this military and feudal ceremony which brought back memories of the old knights in armor.

Thus, by one of the contrasts with which history is filled, — for history is richer in surprises than any play, — it is here, in this famous Gallery of the Mirrors, still full of the pomp and splendor of Louis XIV., whose armies had so proudly crossed the Rhine; here, in this imposing hall, where Lebrun's frescoes represent so many scenes of triumph, that it was given to the Germans to restore the Empire which the French had taken so many ages to overthrow. If the dead retain any interest in human affairs, what must the Great King have thought of the rites just celebrated in his palace?

And the victor himself, what must have been his reflections on the vicissitudes of fate? Even amid all their glory and the intoxication of success, the haughtiest conquerors cannot escape serious thoughts: a secret voice, like that of the slave who kept close to the triumphal chariot in antiquity, whispers into their ears that earthly joys are brief, that the future is uncertain.

Who knows? Despite his prodigious triumphs, the conqueror of Sedan, the all-powerful Emperor William himself had, possibly, his moments of sadness. Possibly he thought more than once, amid all the applause and the blare of trumpets, of that army of which the Abbé Perreyve has spoken, " that army unseen by the corporal eyes, but too clearly visible to the mind's eye, which begins its bloody march . . . the great army of the dead, the army of the slain, the abandoned, the forgotten, the army of cruel tortures and prolonged infirmities, which pursues its fatal march behind what we call glory!" Yes, possibly the conqueror recalled, not without a pang, the time when Germany and France, like two allies, like two friends, took part together in the festivals of peace, in the great ceremonies of modern civilization. Possibly he remembered the time of the Universal Exhibition, when he offered rich bouquets to the Empress Eugénie, when the hospitality of the Tuileries was sumptuous and cordial, when the peoples, fraternized like their sovereigns, and Germans and French, gathered about the same tables, drank Bavarian beer together in the galleries of the joyous palace of the Champ de Mars, while the magic bow of Strauss of Vienna directed the fascinating waltzes, — "The Blue Danube," "Morning Flowers." How many fine and fearless young men, then in the flower and force of their youth, were now sleeping beneath the sods of the battle-field! And how many were wounded and maimed! How many families in mourning, how many mothers in tears! What a sad conflict was this terrible war between two great nations that stood at the head of contemporary civilization, between two intelligent and brave peoples, who were born to understand and to respect one another! And what a price did the unhappy countries, which would have been so prosperous in peace and friendly rivalry, pay for the wars of their emperors and kings!

The day after the proclamation of the Empire of Germany at Versailles, the cannon of Buzenval announced the death agony of Paris. The bombardment of the great capital went on without interruption, and the palace of Saint Cloud began to burn, like a sacrificial pile. The applause which had greeted the new-made Emperor in the Gallery of the Mirrors still continued, when its aspect had swiftly changed. The hall of Triumph became a hospital; thither were taken the Germans wounded at Buzenval. The apartments of the Dauphin, of the Queen, the grand apartments of Louis XIV., were also filled with dying men. The attendants slept in the hall of the Queen's Guards.

The hall of the Grand Couvert — the hall where, in the time of the old monarchy, were given the most magnificent royal banquets, was turned into an apothecary's shop. Cries of pain, long sighs, the death rattle of the mortally hurt, were heard in this splendid gallery, which had so often echoed, in a blaze of lights and flowers, to the joyous music of the ballroom. The wounded, as they lay on their beds of pain, could see above their heads Lebrun's heroic paintings, and possibly to some of them there occurred bitter thoughts about glory; for glory has but a pallid glow to dying men.

Yet the German wounded could at least say that elsewhere, at that moment, there were other wounded and dying men, who were much more deserving of pity. They had the consolation of victory; but the beaten who were wounded, whose pains and sacrifices had been unavailing, who asked, "To what good these heaped-up ruins, these burned huts, so much bloodshed, such devotion, courage, suffering, so many heroic deaths?" Those who died for a country humiliated, defeated, despoiled; those who had lost the flags which might have served for shrouds, what anguish wrung their souls, tortured like their bodies! Alas! how much they needed to press the crucifix to their lips in order not to die in despair.

March 11, 1871, the Germans evacuated Versailles;

they had entered it six months before, September 19, 1870, with drums beating and banners waving. No one would guess what it was that their bands played as they entered the town of Louis XIV. It was the hymn of the Revolution, the "Marseillaise." Yes, by a curious turn of fate, and by a sort of irony, the "Marseillaise," which the French, in the deceptive ardor of their warlike hopes, expected to carry to the other side of the Rhine, was played, not in Germany, but at Versailles, by the bands of King William.

The National Assembly, which had suspended its sittings at Bordeaux, March 11, 1871, had decided to resume them at Versailles on the 20th of the same month. They expected a period of peace. It was fair to hope that after so many sorrows and humiliations, France, mutilated and sorely stricken, would at last enjoy some rest, that its power of suffering was exhausted, that the Niobe of nations was to recover its strength in sadness. But alas! at the very moment when it imagined that it had drunk the cup of bitterness to the dregs, and that it had but to set it down, it was filled anew to the brim, and had to be emptied again.

After the period of fire and blood began the orgy of brandy and petroleum; after the Invasion, the Commune. Mount Valérien continued to thunder; but it was no longer war with the foreigner, but one more terrible and mournful,—civil war. The children of one country plunged into unholy combat; and from the hills which engirdle the capital of capitals, the Germans looked down upon the French murdering one another, like gladiators in a huge amphitheatre.

During the Commune, Versailles presented the strangest appearance. Sometimes the Deputies who could find no quarters used to sleep in the Gallery of the Mirrors, which was transformed by turns into a hospital ward and a dormitory. Stains of blood may still be seen on the floor of this gallery. M. Thiers had installed himself in the house of the Prefect, which had been occupied a few days before by the Emperor William.

From time to time, he would descend the steps to receive the red flags, melancholy trophies of the civil war, which were brought back by the victorious army. By his side was Marshal MacMahon in full uniform. The sound of the trumpet and the roll of the drums was continually heard. At certain points, the town looked like a seat of war; at others, like a watering-place. The Place d'Armes was covered with cannon; and the crowd, when it saw prisoners arrive, did not always display the compassion due to men beaten and disarmed. A little further, and an elegant throng filled the rue des Réservoirs. These fugitives, surprised at meeting one another, used to walk up and down, recounting their experiences, or they would sit at hotel tables, which reminded one of the Conversation Hall at Baden Baden. The spring weather, the lovely evenings, the starlit nights, presented a strange contrast to the savage passions raging in Paris. Nature, which is better than man, seemed to be making a protest by its calm and its unalterable serenity; and the roar of the cannon continually firing was like peals of thunder, startling every one by suddenly breaking forth under a clear sky.

Everybody wondered what would become of the hostages; what would be the end of this lamentable tragedy; what would become of the burning city; would it not be consumed to the last house? Cruel uncertainty! Horrible forebodings! Was it conceivable that such awful things should be going on close to Versailles? As the *Journal Officiel* said, in its number of May 25, "For centuries history has not known such disasters or such crimes." The ancient notion of the power of Fate was exceeded. And yet at Versailles, beside the faces full of alarm, there were faces almost indifferent. I have seen women riding under the trees, and worthy citizens in the park smelling the early perfumes of the flowering lilacs. Tragic incidents make less impression at the moment of their happening than they do when they come back as memories in the imposing remoteness of history.

At the present time,[1] the town of Louis XIV., who held everything that had to do with a parliament in the greatest horror, has become the very heart of par-

---

[1] Written, the reader is reminded, before the return of the French Chambers to Paris. — Tr.

liamentary France; and by another singularity of our time, so fertile in surprises and contrasts, it is the Republic which has chosen this royal town for its capital. In a town which a few years ago was compared to a city of the dead, prevail the warmest discussions, the most tumultuous passions. Thence are sent telegrams all over the world, announcing the agitations of meetings which arouse universal attention.

One moment the Legitimists hoped that in the very theatre where took place the famous banquet of the body-guards, October 1, 1789, — that festival of devotion and loyalty, — they would proclaim the re-establishment of the old monarchy. Providence decided otherwise; and now, in this hall where a Republic was voted by more than one monarchist, there sits a Republican senate. In the other side of the castle, in one of the rooms in the south wing, the Chamber of Deputies holds its meetings. Above the President's chair hangs a picture representing the opening of the States-General of 1789, by Conder. Another odd thing in a Republican chamber is to be seen, — the image of a monarch, and this monarch is Louis XVI.

Sometimes persons who have come to watch the meetings of the Chamber from the galleries, leave the hall and go to meditate in other parts of the palace, in the apartments full of memories of the old monarchy. Nothing so allays the passions of the present as a glance at the past. History is not merely didactic; it is a source of tranquillization.

I never get tired of strolling through the royal apartments, which, strangely enough, were transformed, in 1871, into ministerial offices. For a year, my work-table was placed near Marie Antoinette's drawing-room, in what was called the hall of the Grand Couvert, opposite the picture representing the Doge Imperiali apologizing to Louis XIV. It is there that I conceived for the palace of Versailles a real passion. Having ceased to regard the place as a mere curiosity, I have become deeply attached to it as a shrine where religion and history speak in unison, and where events call forth funeral orations which need no Massillon or Bossuet for their utterance. I have often returned to this historical palace, where the dead have voice and the stones a language to express the hollowness of greatness, the disappointments of vanity, the torments of ambition, the bitterness and emptiness of glory. Seen in its true light, that is to say, in the light of the Gospel, this palace, with its abundant lessons, seems as impressive as a church, and I never enter its gates without a feeling of reverence!

I shall never forget the impression I received one of the last times I visited it. I had just lost a sister who had been the gentle companion of my childhood, the friend of my youth, and I had loved her with all my heart. She died when of the same age as Marie Antoinette, after enduring long sufferings with wonderful resignation. She died like a saint, as an angel might die if angels were mortal. In my grief I wanted to wander through this melancholy palace, whence a plaintive hymn seemed to issue, to remind me, by comparing my homely sorrow with more famous afflictions, that rich or poor, sovereigns or subjects, we are alike condemned to bear the same burden, to empty the same cup of bitterness. On entering the palace courtyard, I saw a multitude near the statue of Louis XIV., on their knees. Priests, sisters of Saint Vincent de Paul, children, were praying and singing. It was the procession which marched, its banner in front, to the three stations of the jubilee, — the Church of Saint Louis, the chapel of the palace, Notre Dame. Then I thought, "How petty are the kings of earth, how great the King of Heaven! Where are the thrones, the crowns, the ashes of the sovereigns who have reigned in this palace? Everything is destroyed, but the cross remains." The singing continued; never did religious music sound to me more holy.

It was as if a mourning country was invoking Divine clemency. It seemed to me that a supernatural band was uniting the quick and the dead, that near these sisters of charity there floated the shades of the heroines of Versailles, of those women who appeased the Divine wrath by innocence or repentance. Yes, I called up all, — the pious Queen, Maria Theresa; and her who exchanged the proud name of Duchess of La Vallière for the pathetic and gentle name of Sister Louise of Mercy; and the haughty Montespan, who was made humble by repentance; the kind Marie Leczinska; and Madame Louise of France, the austere Carmelite; and the two martyrs, Marie Antoinette and Madame Elisabeth. I seemed to hear voices from beyond the grave joining in the litanies.

The procession made its way into the royal chapel, the dome of which, at the side of the palace, is like a catafalque, and where there still lingered the echoes of a sublime voice, the voice of Massillon. Then the faithful entoned the *Miserere*, a song as deep as the ocean, as great as grief; the song of lamentation, of humility to God. I said to myself: "This hymn of penitence must rise to Heaven! Have mercy upon me, O God! according to thy loving kindness. *Miserere mei, Deus, secundum magnam misericordiam tuam.* . . . Make me to hear joy and gladness, that the bones which thou hast broken may rejoice: *Auditui meo dabis gaudium et lœtitiam, et exultabunt ossa humiliata.* . . ." And I raised my heart towards Him of whom Bossuet says, "To Him alone belong glory, majesty, and freedom; the only one who glories in making laws for kings, and in giving them when he pleases great and terrible lessons." Ah! I said to myself, the true end of a study on Versailles is this religious ceremony in the chapel where kings used to kneel. After the crime, reparation; after the pomp of pride, humble repentance; after the wanton favorites, the modest daughter of Saint Vincent de Paul. All France appeared to me like a penitent. No! all these trials and sacrifices were not in vain! The tears and blood were not shed to no purpose! No; a people which has maintained its faith under adversity is not condemned to hopeless decay! Material ruin, and that more terrible thing yet, moral ruin, may be finally repaired. Like Lazarus, France will rise from her tomb; she accepts the lessons of the past, to prepare for the future, and though He has punished her, the God of mercy does not cease to protect her.

INDEX.

Abbaye, the prison of, broken open, 207.
Angoulême, Duchess of, see Madame Royale, 156.
Aubertin, Charles, quoted, 202.

Balls, the last court, at Versailles, 2.
Banquet of October 1 at Versailles, 241.
"Barber of Seville," played at the Little Trianon, 55 et seq.
Bastille, capture of, 211.
Beaumarchais, his efforts to have the "Marriage of Figaro" played, 31; a forerunner of the Revolution, 33; his letter to the Abbé de Calonne, 36; performance of his "Barber of Seville" in the theatre of the Little Trianon, 56.
Besenval, Baron, quoted, 172, 174.
Beugnot, Count, describes Cagliostro's sorceries, 74.
Boehmer, the jeweller from whom the diamond necklace was purchased, 88.
Bombelles, Marchioness of, the friend of Madame Elisabeth, 142.
Bosson, Jacques, Madame Elisabeth's dairyman, 147.
Breteuil, Baron de, orders the arrest of the Cardinal de Rohan, 100.
Brienne, his incapacity, 173; his greed, 176; leaves the ministry, 177.
Broglie, Marshal of, put in command of the troops, 207.

Cagliostro, his appearance in France, 69; attaches himself to Cardinal de Rohan, 70; his charlatanries, 72; banished, 122; his end, 123.
Calonne, his paper proposing to convoke the Notables, 168; his speech in the Assembly, 170.
Campan, Madame, quoted, 24; her interview with Boehmer, 90, 171.
Cazotte, M., prophecies of, 150 et seq.
Chantilly, reception to the Grand Duke Paul at, 27; festivities at, 29.
Chateaubriand describes the pomp of Versailles, 3.
Compardon, M., his book on the diamond necklace, 86.
Condé, Prince of, his courtesy, 28.
Condé, Mademoiselle de, 29.
Court, the French, before the Revolution, 21.

Darboy, Archbishop, his preface to Madame Elisabeth's letters, 157.
Dauphin, the, "asks leave to enter," 14, baptism of, 12; enthusiasm of all classes over, 15 et seq.; illness of, 197; his death, 199.
Diamond necklace, the affair of, 86 et seq.

Elisabeth, Madame, her devotion to Marie Antoinette, 135; her character and life, 136 et seq.; letters of, 142; her religious reflections, 143; her dairy, 147; her imprisonment and execution, 152 et seq.

INDEX.

Elliott, Madame, her account of the Duke of Orleans, 233, 237; tries to induce him to join himself to the King, 238.

Enghien, Duke of, 29.

"Figaro, the Marriage of," its performance prevented, 31; played at Gennevilliers, 35; and at the Comédie Française, 35.

Georgel, Abbé, his zeal in the defence of the Cardinal de Rohan, 110, 120.

Goethe, foresees the Revolution, 125.

Grimm, Baron, quoted, 30, 36.

La Fayette, Marquis of, birth and fortunes, 222 *et seq.*; serves in America, 224; his love of fame, 226; commander of the National Guard, 227; leads the National Guard to Versailles, 229; reassures the King, 256; his course at Versailles, 256; his blind optimism, 260; his sleep, 264.

La Harpe, quoted, 37; his report of Cazotte's prophecy, 151.

Lameth, M. de, ingratitude of, 5.

La Motte, Count de, 78.

La Motte, Countess de, her birth and character, 76 *et seq.*; has an interview with the Cardinal de Rohan, 78; devises her plot against the Cardinal, 79; arranges the mock interview between the Queen and the Cardinal, 84; her plot to obtain the diamond necklace, 91; hears of the arrest of the Cardinal, 102; her defence, 113; her punishment, 123; her death, 125.

Lescure, M. de, *Secret Correspondence* of, quoted, 5.

Louis XVI., delight of, at the birth of the Dauphin, 13; his feeble rule, 163; his weakness and vacillation with the Parliament, 175; decides to convoke the States-General, 177; opens the States-General, 191; a philanthropist and a good man, but not a king, 204; his noble optimism, 205; perceives his errors too late, 209; urges Necker to leave, 209; appears humbly before the Deputies, 214; decides to return to Paris, 215; orders the princes of the blood to leave France, 216; goes to Paris, 219; repels the Duke of Orleans, 239; summoned to Versailles to meet the mob, 248; shows himself to the mob, 265; consents to go to Paris, 267.

Louis XVII. as Dauphin, baptism of, 132.

Louise, Madame, death of, 145.

Mackau, Baroness of, the friend of Madame Elisabeth, 141.

Malouet, his observation on the King's ministers, 202, 204; quoted, 209.

Maria Theresa, her disapproval of private theatricals, 54; complains of the conduct of the Cardinal de Rohan, 62.

Marie Antoinette, at the last court ball no one would dance with, 5; hissed at the Opera, 5; gives birth to the Dauphin, 13 *et seq.*; invites the Baroness d'Oberkirch to her court, 23; her timidity, 24; entertains Gustavus III. at the Little Trianon, 47; her affability at her Sunday balls, 51; her acting at the theatre of Little Trianon, 53; refuses to purchase the diamond necklace, 88; is informed by Madame Campan of the plot, 94; acquitted of any part in the affair, 112; wounded by the verdict, 121; portrait of, by Madame Vigée-Lebrun, 128; death of her daughter Sophia, 129; death of the Dauphin, 131; her rural life at the Trianon, 146; begins to apprehend the impending troubles, 160; her ascendancy over her husband, 172; forbidden to show herself in Paris, 174; her error in favoring the Third Estate, 179; betrayed on every side, 182; her self-possession, 194; evil omens, 196; her anguish at the death of the Dauphin, 199; her partiality for La Fayette, 222; and for the Duke of Orleans, 230 et seq.; realizes the position he has taken, 236; her reception at the banquet of October 1, 243; assailed by calumny, 246; her last visit to the Trianon, 246; rescued by Madame Thibaut, 263; is taken to Paris by the mob, 268.

Marie Louise, visits Versailles with Napoleon, 274.

Maury, Abbé, brings news of the Cardinal de Rohan's arrest to the Countess de La Motte, 102.

Mercy-Argenteau, Count of, witnesses incognito the acting of Marie Antoinette, 54.

Michelet, quotation from, 88.

Mirabeau, a royalist, 203; his famous phrase, 206.

Montreuil, the house of Madame Elisabeth, 139; the dairy at, 147.

Napoleon, his remark about the "Marriage of Figaro," 40; restores the Versailles palaces and the Trianon, 273.

National Assembly, the Third Estate announces itself the, 205.

Necker, has no fears about the States-General, 9; called to the Ministry, 177; assembles the Notables again, 179; deceives himself, 183; the true King of France, 207; gives up his portfolio, 209; opposes resistance to the mob, 250.

Necklace, the diamond, affair of, no longer obscure, 86.

Noailles, Viscountess of, quoted, 7.

Nobility, the French, worthiness of at the period of the Revolution, 7 et seq.; light-hearted and dignified to the last, 11.

Notables, Assembly of, 169.

Oberkirch, Baroness d', on society in France at the period of the Revolution, 10; presented to the Queen, 23; describes Cardinal de Rohan, 66; quoted, 70, 138, 150.

Oliva, d', the, a tool of Countess de La Motte, 82; arrest of, 103; public interest in her, 110; confesses, 113; acquittal of, 119; receives many proposals of marriage, 123.

Orleans, Duke of, organizes the Revolution, 175; exiled to Villers-Cotterets, 176; his relations to the Queen, 230 et seq.; his character, 233; led by circumstances into revolt, 237; repulsed by the King, 239.

Palais Royal, repute of the, 27, 46.

Paris, outbreak of the Revolution in, 209.

Parliament, the action of, 173.

Paul, the Grand Duke, visit of, to Louis XVI., 22; his *bon mot* at the ball, 26; at Chantilly, 27.

Pius VII. at Versailles in 1805, 272.

Poitrine, Madame, nurse of the Dauphin, 15.

Polignac, Duchess of, 214; bidden by the King to depart, 216; leaves Versailles in disguise, 218.

Raigecourt, Marchioness of, dowered by Madame Elisabeth, 141.

Revolution, the, a light affair in the eyes of the nobility, 9; the beginning of, 160 et seq.; insurrection in Paris, 210.

Rohan, Cardinal de, character of, 60; French Ambassador at Vienna, 62; incurs the dislike of Marie Antoinette, 64, 67; appointed Grand Almoner of France, etc., 65 et seq.; his infatuation for Cagliostro, 71; fascinated by Madame de La Motte, 79; in her toils, 81, has a mock interview with the Queen, 84; is duped by the Countess de La Motte into buying the diamond necklace, 92; summoned before the King and examined, 98; arrested, 100; decides to stand trial, 105; protests against lay jurisdiction, 106; shown to have been a dupe, 113; makes his defence, 115; is disgraced by the King, 120; his end, 122.

Royale, Madame, her imprisonment, 156.

Sainte-Beuve, quoted, 37.
Ségur, the Count of, quoted, 45.
States-General, convoked at Versailles, 183; the ceremonies of the assembling, 185; the opening session, 188 et seq.

Taine, quotation from, 3, 7.
Talleyrand, quoted, 9.
Tennis Court, the oath of the, 205.

Tippoo Sahib, embassy of, to France, 197.

Trianon, the Little, the theatre of, 52; Marie Antoinette on the stage of, 53 et seq.; the Queen's last visit to, 246; the fate of, 271.

Versailles, the court theatre at, 2; the pomp of, described by Chateaubriand, 3; localities of the scenes of October 6, 258 et seq.; palace of, entered by the mob, 261; decadence of, 270; Pius VII. at, in 1805, 272; palaces of, restored by Napoleon, 273; visit of, with Marie Louise to, 274; visits of Louis XVIII., Charles X., and Louis Philippe to, 275 et seq.; during the Commune, 289; Napoleon III. and Eugénie's visit to, 278; visit of Queen Victoria and Prince Albert to, 283; Emperor William crowned in the palace of, 285; Museum, creation of, 276.

Vigée-Lebrun, Madame, her picture of Marie Antoinette, 128.

Villette, Rétaux de, arrest of, 103; confesses his part in the affair of the diamond necklace, 113.

www.ingramcontent.com/pod-product-compliance
Lightning Source LLC
Chambersburg PA
CBHW022107230426
43672CB00008B/1306